Visual Secrets

Conveying Messages, Gathering Information and Empowerment in the Age of Social Media

By Yoni Dror

Book 1 in the series "**The Visual Code**"

Phone: +972-52-2807505

Email: yoni@yonidror.co.il

Author: Yoni Dror

Cover and book design: Studio Lev Ari

Professional guidance: Amit Offir

Illustration: Ariel Karmi Dror

Linguistic editing: Odi Lavi and Nataly Shohat

Translation: Hilah Mazyar

Staged photography: Tzuf Karmi Dror

Studio makeup: Roni Sulam

Pictures and photos: Maya Karmi Dror,

Annie Leibovitz, Thomas Hoepker, Greg Kolz, Remi Jouan, Matthew Yohe, Ariel Karmi Dror, Betto Rodrigues, Tinseltown, Peter Bregg, Lev Radin, Joseph Sohm, Krista Kennell, Tzuf Karmi Dror, Peter Souza, Jurvetson, AGIF, Settawat Udom, A. Katz, Media Pictures.pl, Wilhelm Pedersen, Francis Galton, Sotirios Ikonomou, Mustafalive, DelekMotors, Shitzu, Featureflash Photo Agency, rmnoa357, Kevin Gale, U.S. Federal Government, Whitehouse, Kremlin, Russian Government, NASA, Flickr, Wikimedia, Shutterstock

ISBN: 978-1537748160

Table of Contents

For my daughters: Tzuf, Ariel and Roni
For my granddaughter: Naomi
And for Maya, the woman at my side
You are the light illuminating my path.

Preface
And Thanks to Sarkozy

In 1995, I was staying in a remote forest in Princeton, NJ along with a Czech professor, an American photographer, a French art collector and his partner - an English opera singer. I was the youngest of the bunch. I couldn't know then that my life, as I knew it, was about to change forever. Dramatic events, both personal and professional, had driven me to leave my comfort zone and opened gates and doors which I had no idea existed. Of all the temptations offered to me, I chose to enter the gate which led to who I am today - an expert on monitoring information derived from images posted in the social media. This information is crucial to businesses and public organizations, as well as individuals, as it may be the key to understanding the motives, intentions, motivation and ability of your competitors, and enable you to see the bigger picture.

At the end of the third year of my photography and art studies in Haifa, I was asked to be an assistant to a well-known American photographer. I was a promising young man, full of energy and confidence, after winning many international photography competitions. My debut film was sold to a TV channel and featured in several locations as groundbreaking, and the wind at my back was the

America-Israel Cultural Foundation Award for innovation in photography. My future seemed bright at the time.

However, I was young and inexperienced. I paid little attention to this distinguished group I had happened upon. I had nowhere near their ability, experience, knowledge or reputation. Prior to this meeting, I had encountered people of this experience and professional stature only in textbook pages and exhibitions. This group and I - the overzealous young Israeli - stayed in an isolated cabin in the woods for three months, conversing and learning about the meaning of images for mankind. These conversations shook the very foundations of my life. Something great had happened when I realized that I had, literally, only seen a piece of the picture so far.

During one of the weekend workshops at Princeton, Jean-Luc, the French art collector, handed me a photo. Extemporaneously, in front of an auditorium filled with photography students and several big names in the art photography field, he asked, "What do you think?" The photo was of two men standing on a Parisian street, surrounded by multitudes of people. There was a quiet mumbling as the audience fixed all eyes on me. I was surprisingly calm, quiet and confident, considering I had not a clue what I was about to say in the next few seconds. That's what they did in those workshops: threw curve balls during your thesis presentation. I should note that merely one day earlier, I had presented a thesis which wasn't easy to hear; it was subsequently brushed off due to its unpopularity and the fact that the pictures I chose to present failed to support my theory. My thesis was that "the images we choose to present carry within them information about our intentions, revealing that which we do not say. Using these pictures, you can know who's behind their selection and what their true motives and intentions are."

Now I was standing with the photo Jean Luc had handed to me. Two short men looked up at me from the picture. One was smiling, pleased - I recognized him as Jean Luc, the French collector; and the other was unfamiliar, gazing far beyond the frame, dauntless. Even as I heard my own voice, I failed to comprehend where the information was coming from, and how it solved this puzzle (that was how I used to speak at the time, before "The Visual Code" method was accessible to me).

"You're happy and very pleased to be standing near him," I said to Jean Luc, pointing at the man adjacent to him in the photo. "He's reassuring. People, you among them, follow him. He is in the midst of a crisis but is not shaken by it. He is strong, determined, goal oriented..." I wouldn't stop talking. Within a few minutes, I had analyzed the scenario. Finally, upon realizing the man was a politician, I added, "he will undoubtedly go straight to the top." Jean Luc, noticeably excited about the pinpoint analysis, took the photo from my hand and said, "This is my friend, Sarkozy," gesturing to the man in the photo, "and as you said, he will be President of France," he added. This was in the summer of 1995. Twelve years later, the potential recognized in his photo was met, and Sarkozy was elected President of the French Republic.

When that summer ended, I received an offer to stay in New York. It was a generous offer, which could have provided me with a new beginning in New York's creative scene. The temptation was great, but I eventually refused. True to my hunches, I returned to Israel and began my independent research. I believed that people were unaware of the information they revealed in their photos - significant information, which could promote businesses through the understanding of both their customers and competitors.

Online images contain a wealth of information regarding relationships, connections, exact locations, academic degrees, medical conditions, security information, even information that could help solve crimes.

In order to develop both myself and this method, I started acquiring various tools in unusual places; for instance, developing my listening skills. I asked the Program Manager at "Non-Stop Radio" (103 FM) to give me a show where listeners phone in and ask questions about their daily conflicts. I figured that, through the show, an overzealous fellow such as myself could acquire some listening skills. To my surprise, and despite the listeners' inability to see the pictures that were sent to me and analyzed on the show, the Program Manager was convinced. The listening training was successful, and by the time I left the shows seven years later, I had spoken to thousands of people I had never laid eyes on, and could "see" who they were, merely by the sound of their voices. I created an organized template of five personality types, just like in the photos: 'the Philosopher', 'the Achiever', 'the Hedonist', 'the Family Person', 'the Meticulous'. The categories are based on 'the Five Elements' in Chinese medicine and philosophy. **This revealed a distinct connection between visual and auditory recognition, an insight that gave me the confidence and will to carry on.**

At that point, a template had proven itself, through which I could extract valuable information from pictures and other sources. But something was missing, and I didn't know what it was.

A large and prestigious international data collection organization invited me to lecture to its department managers. This was an opportunity to enter the 'lion's den' of data collection and visibility. Aside from the prestige, I was interested in feedback from the top professionals in the field of gathering and analyzing visual information.

The lecture was fluent and successful. When it ended, the person who booked the lecture came up to me, thanked me, and said he believed that I would soon be contacted for further collaboration. Then he disappeared with his friends. I waited. A month, two, three passed - immersed in fantasies of my upcoming breakthrough, finally seeing results and reaping the fruits of my labor. Months came and went, but no one called to invite me, as I had hoped.

In spite of my disappointed expectations, I looked ahead, equipped with my inner passion, and kept at my research; until one day - it happened. Everything suddenly connected. Much like the process I went through n South America[1], I realized that the many distracting images I had pictured in my mind didn't exist outside of it, but were only a figment of my imagination, or something planted there by someone else. Only a small fraction of the images I could see were rooted in actual reality.

However, when I would make decisions based on *real* images, something right, good and accurate would happen. **This was the second time in my life when I could see the big picture.**

I began to see that people aren't interested in photo-based analysis, but rather the added value deriving from it. They want to know how to gather intel about their competitors, how to communicate a message loud enough to increase their sales, etc.; I realized that in order to promote themselves and their business, they needed to improve their **I**mage and capability of sending a clear message. They needed to understand their surrounding environment by **C**ollecting information, all the while going through a process of **E**mpowerment. I started using the acronym **ICE- Image, Collection, Empowerment.**

---

1   See details at the end of this book, in the subchapter "Change your Life's Image by Changing how you See the World – my own case".

After assimilating this insight and sharpening my tools, my customers' results were quicker and more positive.

They were willing to pay more for my service and information, since they were receiving measurable value - their image changed in accordance with the message they wished to convey. They studied their environment by collecting information from pictures that revealed critical intel regarding their competition –the kind of intel that enabled them to accurately characterize competing organizations or expose connections and personal relationships. As they worked, they also went through a process of personal and organizational empowerment.

From the summer of 1995 - the year when analyzing Sarkozy's photo started a revolution within me - to this day, over twenty years have gone by. So far, I have worked mainly with managers, business owners, public and government organizations and countless individuals. Now, I feel the need to share my knowledge with anyone who is interested.

I am hopeful that reading this book will illuminate your path. You can improve the connection between your image and the message you seek to convey, and gather information about your environment through images. This connection will provide you with a powerful tool for recognizing your own personal and professional abilities, and with it, you will be able to see the bigger picture.

I hope you make the most of this book, by moving forward to where you deserve to be.

Yours,
Yoni Dror, 2016

Symbolic statue

Soldier carrying a sword

Work sign
& security personnel

Crowd of women

Nicolas Sarkozy, May 6 2007
Photo: Remi Jouan, Wikimedia Commons

Disclaimer

This book was written for the purpose of sharpening your awareness regarding the importance of the information found within images posted on the internet, particularly in social networks, as well as the importance of using it for your business. The book is not about sophisticated information gathering systems, identity theft, artificial intelligence or social networking. Neither will it teach you how to take a good picture or construct a photo composition. Its main content regards the information which can be found within images and communicated between people; its primary purpose is to provide you with tools and questions that may influence your success, both personally and professionally.

✓ Do you know that your competitors are continuously gathering information about your business, using photos you provide them with?

✓ Do the photos you post serve the message you wish to convey as a business owner?

✓ Have you given any thought to what your profile picture reveals about you?

✓ Are you aware of the business data and personal information reflected in your pictures, prior to posting them?

✓ Do you have an image of success?

This book is meant to provide you with simple tools for collecting and understanding information that your competitors display in the social media. It will help you examine how you look to them, and equip you with the means to improve the messages you seek to communicate through your photos. Furthermore, the book is designed to give you a competitive edge in gathering information, both business-related and personal, in a legal and inexpensive way.

Please note that due to the amount of data which comes from image analysis, the analysis found within these pages is partial, and for illustration purposes only.

This book is the result of my travel down a long road, and an attempt to provide you with a shortcut. Its purpose is to teach you to use the revealed information published by others, thereby being one step ahead of your competitors. In this book, I write about the tool I have designed and still use to this day. These are not rumors or tales of other successful people, but conclusions based on dozens of studies I have read, and data I have gathered and analyzed through thousands of contributions from people over the past 20 years. More than forty thousand people have already been introduced to "The Visual Code" through my lectures, personal counseling and courses. This tool helps create order and an understanding of reality, and provides customers with information crucial to their personal and professional growth.

That being said, this book cannot and will not guarantee your success. I can promise you nothing regarding your personal abilities, or results you may or may not achieve in applying the methods and concepts taught here. Your success depends solely upon your ability to persevere, apply the methods and find the parts best suited for you, using your own knowledge and sound judgment. The tool I have developed will enable you to examine yourself and the way you view and manage situations, and lead you to ask questions before making decisions: Can I see the big picture? How can I look beyond everything that's distracting me, in order to achieve better results?

I hope this book helps you change your life and evolve, both professionally and personally, thereby making you a better person. I thank you for buying it and would love to hear your thoughts about it.

*Please note: the photos in this book are displayed in black and white for technical reasons, although some were originally published in color.

About the Author

Yoni Dror lectures, mentors and shares his unique expertise in understanding precise messages, collecting and analyzing information through images in the media and on social networks. He is also the creator of "The Visual Code" - a diagnostic tool for understanding situations through pictures posted online or sent directly to him for analysis.

The author asserts that people are unaware of the information they divulge about themselves and their business. This information is highly valuable, both in professional and interpersonal fields.

The author is an America-Israel Cultural Foundation laureate for innovation in photography. He considers it his purpose to provide others with the possibility to change their outlooks in order to see the bigger, more complete picture, thereby recognizing the best path for them to take. He fulfills this purpose through his distinctive knowledge in visual information analysis, as well as unique expertise in reading body language.

Yoni Dror believes that there is no 'one size fits all' model of success, and therefore each and every individual should create their own model for reading the images of their lives. This can be done by understanding your inner source, acquiring tools and adapting them to your individual personality.

He started his professional career as a young student. In 1993, he sold his film "The Dream Summer", in which he created a language uniquely for the film. In 1994, the Israeli Educational Television broadcasted a series about Dror - "Using Images as a Unique Tool for Achieving Goals". The series was about his journey as a young Israeli, beginning with his service in a special unit in the IDF and ending with his travels in the jungles of South America.

In 1995, he was chosen for the MoMA (Museum of Modern Art) Cadet Group in New York, and exhibited in the White Gallery. During that year, he stayed at Princeton, participated in "The Meaning of Images for Mankind" photo workshops and conversed with senior lecturers in the field from Europe and the US.

Yoni Dror was a freelance photographer for five years, and in 2000 he became an advisor on using visual tools. He developed various techniques, which served as the steps in constructing "The Visual Code". Throughout the years, he has established himself as a uniquely experienced specialist in the field of analysis through pictures and body language.

Dror has been invited to lecture and teach multiple courses on "seeing outside the box" in various companies, businesses and organizations, national authorities, government agencies and the Presidential Residence.

Dror's methods are highly effective, leading many of his clients to evolve and move forward in their careers by accurately and consistently applying these methods, along with Dror's personal guidance. His love of art and creative thinking has pushed him to seek each of his clients' individual uniqueness, thereby enabling him to customize a tailor-made product for each and every one of them.

Over time, Dror has guided experts, businesses and companies, teaching them to become authorities in their respective fields in order to set them apart from the competition. Dror is considered by many to be a personal and professional mentor, offering his clients a remarkable viewpoint in any given scenario.

A Picture is Worth a Thousand Words

The case of Trump vs. Cruz during the battle between the two Republican candidates for President in 2016, clearly demonstrates how a picture can be used as a dangerous weapon; how powerful, cruel and swift using an image to send a message can be.

It all started with a campaign video published in Arizona, in which there appeared a photo of Melania Trump, Donald Trump's wife, laying naked on a bed in a suggestive pose. The caption: "Meet Melania Trump. Your next First Lady. Or, you could support Ted Cruz on Tuesday." The photo had previously been published in an American magazine, while Melania was cultivating her modeling career.

The originals can be found by typing the caption into the Google search engine.

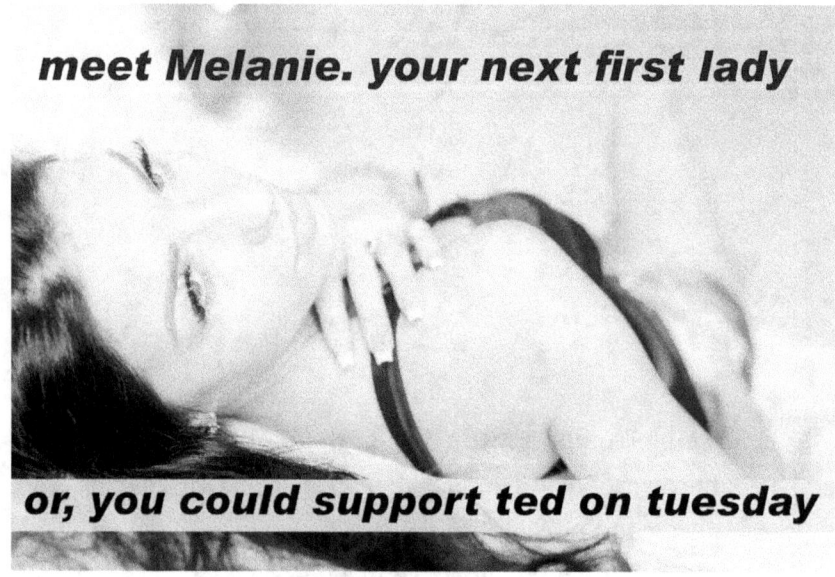

meet Melanie. your next first lady

or, you could support ted on tuesday

Illustration: M.K.D Studio

Photo: Shutterstock

Retaliation wasn't far behind. Trump tweeted a photo of his wife alongside one of Heidi Cruz, Ted's wife, caught in an unflattering pose. He wrote, "The images are worth a thousand words."

Illustration: M.K.D Studio
Photo: Shutterstock

Ted Cruz denied that it was his camp who had published Melania's nude photo; to which Donald immediately replied, "Lyin' Ted Cruz denied that he had anything to do with the *GQ* model photo post of Melania. That's why we call him Lyin' Ted!" When Trump published the photo of angry Heidi alongside glamorous Melania, Cruz reacted: "Donald, real men don't attack women. Your wife is lovely, and Heidi is the love of my life."

As I said, a picture can be used as an aggressive and influential weapon, because the viewer can be manipulated with the image's placement and title. This technique is extensively utilized both in journalism and in advertising. Even if we know that someone artificially placed the images side by side for effect, it can have a tremendous influence on us. Trump's announcement that he wouldn't use that picture again was lip service, as his message was already heard loud and clear; It contributed to the downfall of Cruz's political campaign.

In July 2016, against all odds, Donald Trump was elected the Republican Presidential candidate. His aggressive campaign and use of images to convey his message were keys to Trump's success; as for style - to each his own. After all – that's what democracy is all about.

Chapter One:

The Language of Images

Cave Paintings

Photo: Shutterstock

Everyone Speaks Images

If you are holding this book in your hand, you probably want to learn the rules of the most widely spoken language in the world – the visual language. Fluency in this language will enable you to improve your professional visibility as well as your ability to gather information on the internet, as part of your professional and personal routine. You've most likely seen that learning and attaining information are both abilities which can lead to success. When business professionals meet with me and see the results they receive from photographic materials, they often attribute them to my intuition or various esoteric methods. Though it makes sense for them, they fail to see that the results are rooted in the natural capability each and every one of us has, to pick up on symbols and codes in images.

After a short while of learning to activate their intuitive ability for gathering information, processing it and sending messages using visual codes and symbols, they discover that this ability is a natural part of them. All they had to do was wield it correctly.

A common language is a prerequisite for achieving any goal, and the drive behind mankind's unprecedented achievements. Paintings dated forty thousand years ago, discovered in caves, testify that people communicated and sent messages to one another using symbols and visual themes. Professional, cultural and political communities survived because they had a common language through which they formed groups with similar goals.

For five hundred and forty million years, nature has been developing a sophisticated visual processing mechanism connecting the eyes with the brain. This mechanism is key to understanding the language of codes and icons created by humanity, beginning with paintings, sculptures and various symbols. The invention of cameras and photography, over two hundred and fifty years ago, accelerated visual language development and broadened human communication. Photos were easily printed, and were considered a reliable alternative to paintings, as they reached the viewer without the artist's filters. Photos served as indisputable evidence of events, and proof that the value of sight far exceeds that of words.

In today's global village it is difficult to communicate homogenously, since we speak hundreds of languages, use thousands of dialects and come from varied cultural backgrounds.

Fast-paced technological developments have created many different communication platforms: Google+, Instagram, Facebook, WhatsApp, LinkedIn, Pinterest, MySpace and many others. One of the most prominent platforms is Facebook. If Facebook were a country, it would be the most populated country in the world. These means of communication connect people from different cultures who have common economic and social interests, but do not speak the same language. This is what created the need to choose a language which brings different cultures together – a fast, intuitive language which would be simultaneously understood in Shanghai, in New York and in Buenos Aires.

As a result, half of the world's population is already making connections and sending messages, both personal and professional, 24/7, 365 days a year, through a network that never sleeps. **Pictures and videos are the preferred method of communication.**

Two major statistics reflect the power of the visual language: every day over a billion pictures are uploaded to the social media, and every minute over three hundred hours of videos are published on YouTube alone.

Many business owners are unaware of these figures and keep doing what most people do when they wish to increase their customer traffic: build expensive websites and create ineffective campaigns. **The last thing your customers will do, if that, is enter your homepage.** Many people consider homepages to be unreliable, since they contain what *you* write about *yourself*. Most of your customers are on social networks; communicating, conveying messages through pictures and videos, browsing and collecting information they find interesting.

Intuitive Human Ability

Pictures and videos are an effective means of conveying personal and marketing messages and steering public opinions. However, alongside its effectiveness, images may also be a devastating tool against you and your business. I encounter a gross amount of information through people's uploaded photos on a daily basis: professional info, personal info, intel regarding partners and products, as well as personal and professional relationships. **The goal of this book is to make you aware and push you to action – today.**

Learning to understand the effects of images gains you an edge for your business. You can figure out your competition's motives and intentions; you can plant hidden messages in your photos, to influence your customers. You can bypass the multi-language difficulty and communicate through one international language that everyone can understand.

In my lectures, I show photos of real people and actual events from my database, which contains thousands of photos that have been sent to me. I promise the audience that by the time the lecture is over, they will know how to discover information and messages hidden within pictures, such as intent, motive, conflict and valuable business intel on their competitors.

After many years of lecturing and teaching, I have seen audiences succeed in extracting information out of photos within an hour of being exposed to how it can be found. This is not because I am an outstanding instructor, but because understanding images is an **intuitive human ability**, though many fail to see it as an efficient tool available to them.

Revealed and Concealed Messages

Every picture can be divided into two, not always equal, parts. Much like an iceberg, whose tip you can see, hinting at its greater mass which remains hidden from view.

The revealed part, in a profile picture for example, is the initial factor you had intended for the viewer to notice. It represents the viewer's first impression and is meant to bring about the desired effect. For instance, if you have chosen to wear glasses, a hat, a business suit, a bathing suit, be in a certain location or with an additional person in the photo – whoever sees it will understand that you have consciously chosen to display those elements within the picture, and will subsequently come to certain conclusions. This part is your membership card, representing the club you are (or want to be) part of. It will determine whether a customer begins a purchase process or moves on to your competition. **This impression is created in less than one second.** Make sure that it reflects what you represent, in the blink of an eye.

Steve Jobs chose to launch the new iPhone wearing a black, Chinese shirt. In Eastern culture, the color black represents strength, power, and new beginnings.

- Do you think he chose it consciously?
- Is this a nod to the huge population of China and India? (Consider the ongoing competition between Apple and Samsung.)
- Could it reflect his spiritual connection with Asian culture?
- Does it reflect his fashion sense?

Which of the above do you suppose is correct?

Steve Jobs had extraordinary awareness. So we can conclude it was a conscious choice. The picture reflects his cultural tendencies and sense of style. Asian viewers can easily relate to someone who is dressed like them. If a man walks into a synagogue without a yarmulke, he will draw attention to himself and generate antagonism. If he wears the yarmulke, he will blend into the crowd as part of it.

I believe all of the points above are correct, even if some remain publicly unspoken.

Revealed message: "this is what we're here for"

Concealed message: clothing or an object hinting to a lifestyle (Asian attire)

**Sending a message in under 1 second –
Steve Jobs presenting the iPhone 4 in 2010.
Minimum details, in the spirit of Apple**

On a daily basis, I come across discordant photos which fail to reflect the message they are meant to convey, in social networks. For instance, a dissonance between the person's appearance in the photo and his profession.

Below is an example of such a profile picture. **Can you guess this man's profession by this photo?**

Clearly, an investment advisor…
An example of a bad profile pic
Photo: Shutterstock

On the other hand, here is a profile picture where the message or profession match the actual photo:

A professional portrait exhibiting her occupation
Photo: Maya Karmi Dror

The message or hidden information in the profile picture is the second stage of observation. More often than not, the viewer won't perceive it, but will be able to feel the milieu reflected in the photo. Upon closer observation, there is a lot of information to be discovered from within the hidden message: whether the photo is old or new; who and what appear in it; the angle; the photo's composition; the dominant colors. Information can be derived from the background, street signs, symbols, diplomas, family photos, even a doctor's referral hanging on the fridge.

Giving away unnecessary information.
(Note the background info on the refrigerator)
Photo: Tzuf Karmi Dror

Additional information can be extracted from your body language. It is a rule of thumb that our bodies are positioned in unison with our emotional states. Tilting one's head or shoulder, choosing a withdrawn or open stance, looking directly at the camera or elsewhere – are all affected by the emotional state. Due to a considerable amount of time spent watching screens and absorbing visual information from movies, TV and computers, people have developed the impressive capability of reaching instant conclusions about characters by extracting information from images. In other words, the ability to get information from pictures is a natural result of dozens of years spent internalizing visual messages.

Confident body language.
Actor Robert De Niro's Handprint Ceremony, L.A.
Photo: Betto Rodrigues, Shutterstock

Images are made up of many layers of information, two of which are paramount: the subject and the background. When people look at photos on Facebook, they view the profile picture and cover photo as one piece. The profile picture and cover photo should complement each other and support the message we wish to convey, as if they were one single image.

The profile picture is the "you" that you wish to display, in accordance with the role and the identity you represent; and the cover photo should support your profile picture by creating the appropriate setting.

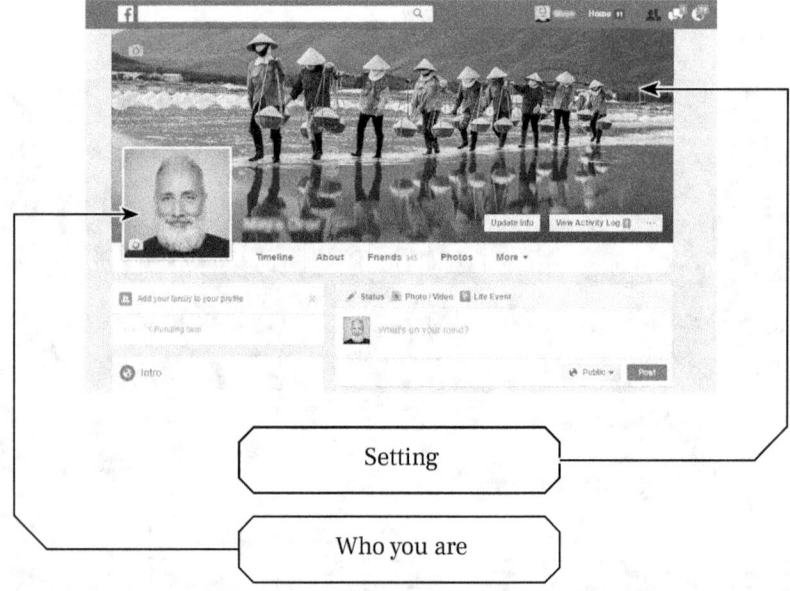

Your profile picture and cover photo should support your message.
Illustration: MKD Studio
Photos: Shutterstock

Advertisers and PR firms were the first to see the potential in filling the frame with marketing messages.

Benicio Del Toro in "The Wolfman" premiere

Photo: Tinseltown, Shutterstock

Concealed or Subliminal Messages

A subliminal message is a signal or datum which is designed to enter our consciousness without our notice. Subliminal messages are transmitted through photos and sounds which appear for an instant, thus leaving the receiver unaware, while successfully entering the viewer's mind. The impact of a subliminal message can be particularly powerful, as the person exposed to it cannot choose to consciously respond, react or express opposition to the message received.

This type of messaging used to be common in advertising and propaganda, for instance, in election campaign broadcasts. Many conspiracy theories assert that experimentation in subliminal message transmissions proved successful in influencing viewers, and made them act according to the short stimulations to which they were exposed. That being said, evidence is yet to be found that subliminal messages can in fact influence specific choices made by those exposed to them. Still, there is some data to support the claim that exposure to subliminal messaging results in short-term, built-in effects.

The most obvious example of the impact of subliminal messages is an experiment[2] in which the participants were exposed to national icons.

In Israel, this revealed that exposure to the Israeli flag made participants' political opinions more moderate compared to their previous views.

---

2   "Subliminal Exposure to National Flags Affects Political Thought and Behavior", PNAS. Authors: Ran R. Hassin, Melissa J. Ferguson, Daniella Shidlovski and Tamar Gross

Governor Andrew Cuomo at the Israel Parade, NY 2014
Is the viewer affected by the flag's presence?
Photo: Lev Radin, Shutterstock

The same research also showed that American participants tended to identify more profoundly with the American value system after being subliminally exposed to distinc American symbols.

Air Force One is one of the most prominent symbols of American Presidency.
The Presidential Aircraft inspired several Hollywood movies.
Photo: U.S. Federal Government, Military-Air Force, Wikimedia Commons.
PD-USGov, License

Presidential podium

Donald Trump during his campaign in Sacramento, 2016.
In the background, his plane, resembling Air Force One
Photo: Joseph Sohm, Shutterstock

The photo shows Donald Trump speaking at an election rally, against a backdrop of a plane resembling Air Force One. Trump is implanting the viewer with the thought that he is already President. By Election Day, the voters will already have visualized him as President, making it easier for them to vote for him.

Have you ever considered why, in election rallies, candidates have their backs to the crowd, rather than facing it?

It's because frames serve as advertisement space, used to convey messages and ideas. The audience and symbols in the background enhance the message for the viewers.

Hillary Clinton at an election rally, NY 2016.
Her campaign slogan is displayed by "extras" in the background
Photo: Krista Kennell, Shutterstock

Photos of Leaders and the Messages Therein

Let's analyze, for example, American President Barack Obama's photos vs. Russian President Vladimir Putin's photos. These two leaders from different cultures use messages adapted to their respective cultures. When Russia wishes to send a message using their leader, he will usually be featured alone, mostly outdoors. When America wishes to send a message using their leader, he will be surrounded by a crowd, his family members, or American icons in the background. The symbols within the photos reflect the values and culture of the photo's target audience.

Let's start with Obama.

Obama's official photos, as displayed in the media, reflect American values. Below, you can see the American flag on the left side of the photo and the Great Seal flag on the right. The President stands in the center, flag pinned to his lapel, watch on his left wrist (as is customary) and the presidential desk behind him.

The photo reflects a conservative world, driven by traditions and a respect for symbols. The President's body is "touching" the two larger symbols – the American and Great Seal flags – and his head is framed in an "aura" (the window), a sign of hope, and primarily of the Christian faith (in Christian icons, an aura around a person's head symbolized their power and righteousness).

Concealed message:
a Christian aura

The Great Seal flag

The American flag

President Barack Obama's official White House portrait
Photo: Peter Souza, The White House
License PD-USGov-POTUS Wikimedia Commons.

In the next photo, we see Barack Obama and his wife, Michelle, waving to the crowd as they descend the stairs of a temple-like building. Significant American national symbols decorate the photo. On the left, the Vice President and his wife stand in waiting for Obama, adding to the photo's impact and emphasizing the American values presented here.

Barack and Michelle Obama at the 2009 Presidential Inauguration
Photo: Jurvetson, Flickr. Wikimedia Commons, CC-BY-2.0, License

The third photo, which depicts the President surrounded by his family, is meant to reflect family values - the heart of the American belief system.

Official White House photo of President Barack Obama and his family.
Their hands shed light on their family ties.
Photo: Annie Leibovitz, The White House
PD-USGov, License. Wikimedia Commons

Now, let's take a look at Vladimir Putin, the President of Russia, and try to see why he is often partially clothed in his photos.

Vladimir Putin is regularly photographed bare-chested while fishing, hunting, flying or on horseback. His sturdy, exposed image is used to convey several messages, reviewed below.

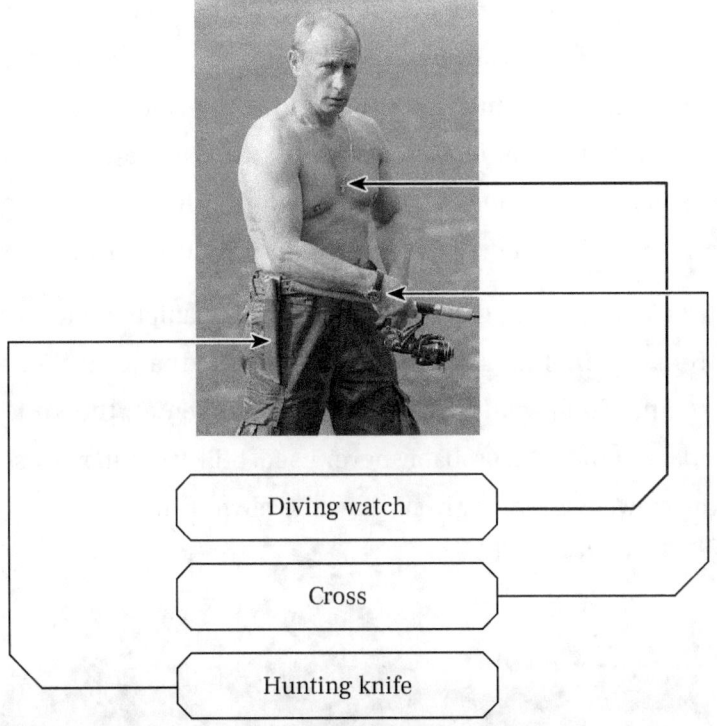

Vladimir Putin, fishing on a river

In this photo, Putin looks directly at the camera. Someone made sure we notice several symbols which convey clear messages, such as the cross around his neck (Orthodox Christian), the diving watch on his right wrist (mysterious), the fishing rod (outdoorsy), the hunting knife (rugged) and the camouflage pants (military).

The message: his dead-on gaze conveys confidence and honesty. His bare chest combines strength and tenderness. It says: 'I am not afraid to be exposed. I have nothing to hide'. The contrast against the river in the background makes him look powerful. He is exposed, yet invulnerable.

What does it say about the Russian perception of a leader? Perhaps Russians use simple, universal symbols which are recognizable to everyone (nature, hunting and rivers) rather than the official Russian symbols, because Russia's current icons are still relatively new and have yet to be assimilated in the public's mind. The old icons, those of the former Soviet Union, represent an old, corrupt and primitive world.

When closely examining the photo, the viewer manipulation becomes apparent: Putin's hair hasn't moved, unlike that of a hunter or fisherman, which would have been more unkempt; the knife and holster are brand new, probably never used. Still, you can rest assured that the viewer will willingly swallow the obvious bait.

Vladimir Putin – hunter and combat soldier
Photo: The Russian Government.

In the second photo, Putin, dressed as a soldier or hunter, is intently pointing a rifle at an unknown target. The image is powerful because we cannot see who or what Putin is targeting. It could be an animal, a dissident, or even a country (the actual story is that Putin is shooting a tranquilizer dart at a tiger, but even if the viewers are aware of that fact, the image etched in their minds is: Putin - the sharpshooter).

The viewers are free to guess, and you can bank on Putin steering them towards his agendas.

In the third photo, the Putin family is sailing. Even in the family portrait, the president prefers sending a message through nature.

Official Kremlin portrait of the Putins, 2002.
Once again, Putin favors pictures taken outdoors.
Photo: Kremlin, Wikimedia Commons. CC-BY-4.0, License

Russia encompasses a tapestry of ethnic groups; it is dealing with an economic crisis and searching for its lost superpower status. In order to return to its former glory, Russia needs a strong and dynamic leader that no one dares challenge, and nothing sends the right message quite like the right photo.

In summation, the comparative photo analysis of two presidents who represent different cultures – USA vs. Russia – illustrates that revealed and concealed messages vary between cultures (national icons vs. symbols in nature), in accordance with the needs and nature of the target audience.

Local and Global Symbols in Pictures

Through theatres, TV and the internet, hundreds of millions of people are constantly exposed to movies and images which contain symbols and codes. These icons have been ingrained, over time, through widely recognizable cultural works, from best-selling books such as "Alice in Wonderland", to blockbusters like "Rambo". Apart from the *global* symbols, there are *local* visual languages, such as national symbols, or icons relevant to smaller groups. For example: In Western culture, dogs represent loyalty; foxes – wisdom; sheep – adaptability; Nazis and swastikas – evil.

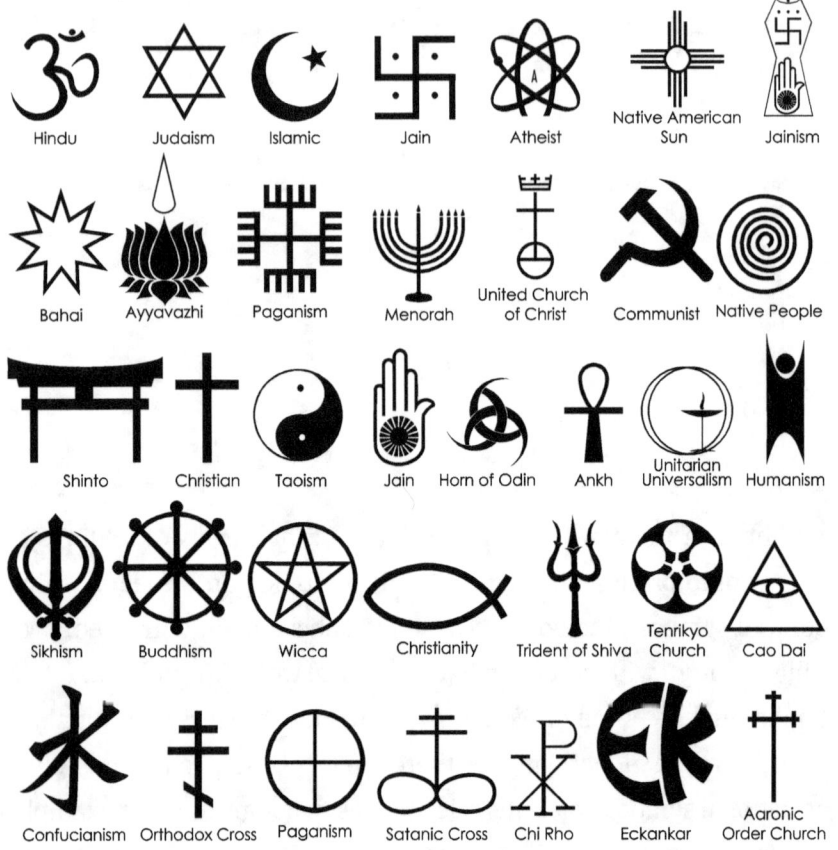

Photo: Shutterstock

Israel's shadow

One of the primary things I noticed while visiting Adina's place of business were the maps. A map of Israel was plastered on almost every single wall. So, it came as no surprise when the photo she chose to show me contained the same shape. When I pointed it out to her in her photo – a shadow in the shape of Israel – she was surprised, but immediately understood and told me about her relationship to maps.

Below is the photo. To Israeli eyes, the shadow's resemblance to the map of Israel is easily noticeable.

Israel's Shadow
Photo: courtesy of the subject, Ms. Adina Mor

A Flag on the Moon

Here is a photo with international symbols. Looking at it, you may recall the sentence which goes with it: "That's one small step for man, one giant leap for mankind." When American astronaut Neil Armstrong, first set foot on the moon on July 21, 1969, it was a universally defining human event, and Armstrong became famous as the first man to ever walk on the moon.

'That's one small step for man, one giant leap for mankind'
Astronaut David Scott, Apollo 15 Commander,
saluting the American Flag on the surface of the moon.
Photo: NASA, Shutterstock

Images as Effective Persuasion

When lecturing, I ask the audience which of their belongings they would salvage if their house were on fire. For most people, the answer is definitive – photo albums. It's interesting to think that, in a stressful and panic-filled situation, we choose our photos over other personal property. The power of pictures comes from the significance we give them. They are our way of capturing memories, connecting with others and remembering them. Photos are a testament to human existence and a representation of our reputation.

Photos serve as a testament, as indisputable evidence, the impact of sight far exceeding that of words. Pictures effect our emotions and move us to action. They're a statement – freezing a moment in time and expressing a given situation. They affect our consciousness. They are the most widely spoken universal language, connecting people who speak different tongues.

Collecting information and investing in the image of businesses used to be the exclusive privilege of huge corporations who have massive budgets. This tool provided such corporations with a significant edge over any competitors, giving them unlimited control. Now, due to the social network and Smartphone revolution, anyone can gather information in a legal, cost-free way, anytime, anywhere. It is only natural that your customers review information about both you and your competitors, prior to making a purchase.

Today, we know that images have a fast, effective impact on customers. Given the fact that images contain symbols and codes which affect our emotions, the information contained within them is not always rational, making it more powerful. The right message reflected in a photo can serve as the catalyst for a customer's decision to contact you.

Most business owners fail to use images in a correct and effective manner. They are unaware of the message images can convey, and the multitudes of information within them. Understanding the rules of the visual language is a prerequisite to professional success.

As a business owner, you can send a message that serves you, using a certain photo. You may want to express a state of mind (fear, joy, envy) or a concept (freedom, art, equality).

Dog and baby
Photo: Shutterstock

According to the cliché, the best sellers are dogs and babies. So why not both?

When you wish to convey growth, hope etc., the message you should be sending is an emotional one. Emotional symbols are personal, and it is therefore important to find symbols which touch many people. Political, religious, sports or cultural symbols can also be added.

Nothing conveys emotion as quickly as a religious symbol.
Photo: Shutterstock

The sales power of the Messi brand is common knowledge.
Photo: AGIF, Shutterstock

Using the right photo in the right place tells the viewer that you, the website or business owner, have an understanding of the path and the vision to which you wish to lead your customer. In order to emphasize the message, add a small caption, such as "Freedom", "Loyalty", "Creativity", "The Road to Success", "The Dream – an Apartment in the City" etc.

How One Photo Caused a Scene - *a case study*

The World Trade Center burning down
Photo: personal courtesy of the photographer Thomas Hoepker

This is a photo by Magnum Agency's photographer, Thomas Hoepker, depicting New Yorkers sitting in the sun, as the Twin Towers burn in the background (September 11, 2001).

The photo was taken on the day of the tragedy, from the other side of the Brooklyn Bridge, but it was only published five (5!) years afterwards. Hoepker waited because he believed that the photo was unworthy of being part of the dramatic visual testimony that had flooded America and the entire world at the time. He chose not to publish the photo immediately, due to his patriotism and solidarity with the nation's grief.

What is it we actually see here?

A bunch of young New Yorkers, sitting and chatting on a normal, sun-bathed Brooklyn day. Behind them, across blue waters and under cerulean skies, a huge cloud of smoke and dust rises over Manhattan, where the Twin Towers stood before being struck by two passenger planes, causing their collapse. Nearly 3,000 people were killed that day. The New Yorkers are sitting at a comfortable viewpoint, pleasantly chatting, seemingly having a relaxing afternoon, completely oblivious to this urban and national disaster. No one is even glancing at it.

Some of the young people photographed wrote protest letters, claiming that they were stunned by the event and found comfort in their togetherness because they *did* care. As I said, all this had happened five years after the fact. We may never know the truth, like many other answers regarding both important and unimportant questions.

Why did the photo cause such a scene? Let's analyze:

In the picture's foreground sits a group of American teenagers. The bike, which brought one of them there, is between them. Soon, the bike's owner will most likely get back on it, heading towards the rest of his life. The youngsters sit near the water. **Their body language is relaxed; they're leaning, some forward and others backward; three of them are defiantly, or disinterestedly, ignoring the ongoing tragedy. They're facing each other with their backs to it.** Only two of them are watching the occurrences behind the others' backs, out of which only one seems troubled, judging by his tense crouching position. The ambiance in the photo is leisurely: blue waters, landscaped bushes, smiling faces, a friendly chat in a social gathering, wherein the participants are untroubled with the scene taking place in the background. **Allegedly, there is a distinct cognitive dissonance here:** serenity against the backdrop of tension, apathy in the face of disaster – psychologically, these are very difficult to accept.

Or perhaps it is the physical distance between the occurrence and the group, much like the distance between a combat pilot and the city he's bombing – the physical remoteness distances him from dealing with the destruction he's causing.

Tools for Photo Analysis

When analyzing a photo, we must pay attention to many different components: whether the photo is in color or in black and white, geometrical or amorphous shapes; its composition, date, background, cropping and altering, etc.

For example: color has a physiological effect on the eyes, and its meaning is culture-dependent. In China, for instance, the color white represents death and grief, whereas in the west, these things are represented by black.

Here's a tip: if you want to do business with the Chinese – refrain from wearing white.

In Asian culture, white is the color of separation.
A goodbye ceremony for Lor Sae Yuk, who died at age 102. Thailand, 2013
Photo: Settawat Udom, Shutterstock

Thousands of cops and friends accompany the family members of
rian Moore, the murdered police officer, 2015.
Photo: A. Katz, Shutterstock

Because it used to be a rare color, purple represents nobility. Women in red represent sex and danger. Blue affects creativity, and yellow is the color of confidence and optimism.

More details on this subject can be found in Chapter Four: **From Theory to Practice.**

Chapter Two:

Pictures in Our Heads

Photo: Shutterstock

Mind Over Matter

I n 1922, American Pulitzer Prize winning author and journalist, Walter Lippmann, described the phenomenon of images which exist in our minds. "Pictures in our heads", he called them, claiming that our brains are overflowing with mental pictures of our loved ones, other people and events. These pictures reflect our thoughts, goals, needs and relationships, and shape our public opinions.

A small portion of the pictures in our heads stem from real life experiences. In most cases, we create images of events without experiencing them firsthand, but rather hearing about them from other sources – mostly media. Sometimes the pictures in our heads cause irrational opinions to be formed, because they are generated as a reaction to a false reality.

Lippmann was among the first to predict the direction in which the world was going – using symbols, codes and metaphors in order to promote businesses and public agendas. These means used to be the exclusive privilege of ad-men and publicists, who knew how to choose images which would create emotions, consensus or frustration, at the sight of a shapely woman, a shiny car or a group of young people jumping around happily, drinking the nectar of youth.

Today, anyone can create an independent campaign for promoting and increasing sales. As a business owner, you can easily promote your product by knowing what pictures are in your customers' heads. Effective communication with your target audience will be obtained by creating an image which connects them, through which you can convey a message.

Car Advertisement - Pictures Speak Louder than Words

Ford, for instance, utilized the human trait of remembering images better than words. It advertised two adjacent ads in the media. The viewer will remember the picture, not the text.

The first ad - "A thousand words"

Photo: courtesy of Ford

The second ad – "A picture"

Ford **MONDEO**

תמונה אחת

Photo: courtesy of Ford.

The 'Picture' That Won Him the Nobel Prize

In 1969, journalist Gabriel Garcia Marquez was on his way to a family vacation in Acapulco. As he pondered his decision to retire following his literary failures, he suddenly had an epiphany. In his mind's eye, he saw the detailed image of the book he had wanted to write since his youth. Without delay, he turned his car around, went home, shut himself in his room and did nothing but write. To do so, he quit his job as a journalist, leaving his wife to deal with the creditors and debtors that came knocking on their door.

After 18 months of walling himself in, shutting the world out and forfeiting a family life (or any life at all), he finally exited his room, pale and emaciated, holding a bundle of over thirteen thousand pages in his hand. The book "One Hundred Years of Solitude" was published in 1967 and forever changed the face of global literature. In 1982, Gabriel Garcia Marquez won the Nobel Prize in literature.

Later, Marquez shared about the defining moment in which he visualized the book's exact image, which became his beacon during the long writing process.

What's the Picture in *Your* Head?

VC Zanit Kazan win the 2015-16 CEV Champions League
Photo: MediaPictures.pl, Shutterstock

The pictures in our heads are a constantly moving database. They directly affect our decision-making process, and can be used as leverage or fuel for realizing our dreams and desires, analyzing where we are and identifying where we wish to be.

Here is a simple exercise for unveiling the pictures in your head. If you do it properly, you'll be surprised with the result.

Read the questions and describe a specific picture for each one. Write your answers on a piece of paper. Don't take more than five seconds to think about each question before writing. After reading each question, you can either close your eyes or keep them open – whichever works for you.

- What image comes to mind when you hear the word "success"?

- What image comes to mind when you hear the word "family"?

- What image comes to mind when you hear the word "failure"?

- What image comes to mind when you hear the word "destination"?

- What image comes to mind when you hear the word "impossible"?

- How many of the images you saw actually happened in your reality, and how many belong to a false reality (for instance, pictures you've seen in the media)?

Below are some examples from my experience as a mentor and analyst. When I asked one of the coachers I worked with to choose a picture that defines her, she selected a picture of Hillary Clinton. "She's a success story, and that's how I would like to see myself," she said. This phenomenon, where people choose to show or describe themselves using someone else's photo, is quite common. People who see their success through photos of others are an example of how people distance themselves from success by attributing it to others.

When people are asked to choose their success picture, they will mostly select a photo of their children or family. That's why we mostly don't see *ourselves* as part of our success pictures.

On the other hand, when people are asked to choose their failure picture, they will usually **see themselves in it**.

To summarize, it is my experience that most of the pictures described will have nothing to do with real life experiences. They mostly come from an external source: TV, internet, movie theatres. The human brain is like a sponge: it can absorb all kinds of ideas, which is why working at choosing the right mental image can be extremely effective.

Chapter Three:

Gathering Information on Social Networks - Rules & Background

Photo: Shutterstock

How do your family's profiles affect your business?

Would you divulge your innermost secrets to a stranger? Would you reveal your personal and professional relationships? Would you let your competitors in on privileged business intel? Probably not. We intuitively share our secrets with very few people. That's why it may come as a surprise when I tell you that **you are unintentionally sharing your personal and professional secrets through the photos you and your acquaintances share in the social media.**

As I've mentioned earlier, pictures and videos are effective key ways of conveying messages that will change personal, marketing and public opinions. While effective, they can also be a destructive tool, a double-edged sword for you and your business. Every day, I come across mountains of information that people give away along with their photos – business intel, personal info, revealing partners and products, personal and professional relationships.

Therefore, the purpose of this book is, on the one hand, making you aware of the financial possibilities deriving from both advertising and collecting information through photos; and on the other hand, getting you to stop uploading images without examining them first.

People view social networks as a legitimate method of making contacts, catching up with old friends, finding love or a new job, or mere boredom relief. But are you aware of the information that you or your family members divulge in the photos you post? They contain personal information about relationships, conflicts, your personality, business contacts, intents and motivation. Therefore – beware!

Gathering and Analyzing the Competition's Tactical Information - *case studies*

Sarah and Daniela - from Competition to Collaboration

Daniela, a partner in a successful law firm, told me in a burst of candor: "Every time I look at Sarah's (a competing advocate) Facebook, I am completely consumed with jealousy." She pointed to a photo on Sarah's wall and added, "How does she manage to lecture in all those conferences?!" Daniela also told me that a close friend of hers, in the spirit of new ageism, suggested that she "simply stop looking at her page." "No way," I said, realizing the potential for Daniela within Sarah's profile. "You're simply looking at the wrong things. Rather than ignoring her Facebook, you should look more often. Sarah's professional page is an informational goldmine for your business. If you recognize what it is about her business page that agitates you, you will recognize what yours is missing. You might even end up sending her flowers," I joked, not realizing how right my prediction was.

Since her competitor uploaded many unfiltered photos, the material analysis gave quick results. In a lot of the pictures Sarah had posted on

Facebook, we could easily recognize some of the conference participants. A quick analysis resulted in a group diagnosis. Daniela came to see two facts: (a) the people in the group were inextricably linked to Sarah's firm; (b) Sarah could not provide them with the consultation they required in a certain field, in which Daniela was an international expert.

Daniela found the information derived from the social network encouraging, and said she intended to launch an aggressive marketing campaign targeted at the people in the photos. I told her that collaborating would be both wiser and more lucrative. Fortunately, Daniela took my advice. After meeting with Sarah, her competitor, a collaboration regarding a comprehensive product designed for senior executives was formed.

I was happy to learn that Daniela and Sarah had come to understand the immense potential of online business information. Today, they routinely gather information as part of their workday, and Sarah has stopped giving away unfiltered information about her business through images.

Social networks have changed the world. Most of the power that was thus far in the hands of written and digital media now belongs to each and every one of us. The potential in the connection between social media and imagery comes from social networks serving as a reliable source of information, due to the fact that the people behind the profiles are the ones providing the information about themselves, selecting the pictures they post. Images, as mentioned, are a reliable source of information for the viewer.

That being said, we must also consider that various entities are tempted to abuse the online information. There have been many cases of misusing information obtained from social networks.

The Startup's Information Leakage - *a case study*

During a meeting with two partners in a startup company, I was asked to prepare a preliminary report regarding the company's information leakage through social networks. Finding the information was easy: one of the company's employees posted a photo of a bunch of people from the company's day out on Facebook, along with the name of the project they were working on. To top it off, the employee congratulated one of the participants on his relocation.

When meeting again, the partners were astonished by the information I had gathered about their main project, most of the employees who were assigned to it, and the manager who had relocated to Canada (most likely to work on another project). The guy who uploaded the information to Facebook did so innocently, not considering for a moment that he was giving away privileged information that would prove extremely valuable to his company's competition. The competitors had been served information regarding the project developed by the startup, its geographical distribution and the people behind it, on a silver platter.

Sometimes an innocent photo you post will serve as valuable intel for your competitors. Photo: Shutterstock

After presenting the information I had extracted from the social network to the partners, including names, project locations, and even information regarding a new customer that the competitors might consider stealing from them, it became clear to all that we had to act quickly to fix the breach. That very day, one of the team managers was given the responsibility of defense against data leakage in social media.

Getting Inside Your Competitor's Head

So far, most information gathering has been tactical, relying on the information published by your competitors and comments on their content. Today, by utilizing tools for collecting information from uploaded photos, you can get inside your competitors' heads and follow their thought process.

Nowadays, 80%-90% of the companies require online information classification. This is true for security organizations such as the military and Ministry of Defense, as well as for commercial companies that are exposed to competition, such as banks, advertising companies, the food industry and more. If a bank decides to provide its business clients with a new service and a competing bank discovers that decision on an employee's Facebook page, the information serves the competition. This is true for every company that has competitors and whose employees divulge detailed information online regarding any aspect of their work.

After examining what the "classified information" is according to the company's management, I bring up the risks, telling them that this information can reach competitors through social networks.

Sometimes I see recommendations to cut off the company's computers from Facebook; but that's irrelevant, since everyone has a Smartphone. Rather than cutting them off, I recommend enhancing the organizational awareness amongst employees – teaching them the difference between what is permitted and what is prohibited on the one hand, and how to use social media for promoting the business after hours on the other hand.

Utilizing the information revealed in social networks for your business is not illegal, but there are those who use the information illegally, for sting operations or identity theft.

I have often met businesspeople who have Facebook and LinkedIn profiles, but do not update them often, as they are (justly) worried about business intel leakage. I advise these people to decide whether they are "in" or "out". If someone wants to gather information about you, they will start with your family's / friends' pages, knowing that you have no control over the information leaked from other people's accounts. In the age of social networks, you cannot hide; and as a business owner, you cannot completely control the people or entities publishing information that may reveal intel about you and your business.

On the other hand, you *can* control the images *you* choose to post. Therefore, it's better if you upload pictures containing the messages you wish to convey. Please note that fictitious images containing misleading information can be posted from time to time in order to confuse your competitors. Remember: the pictures you upload are regarded as reliable, firsthand reports.

One of the greater advantages that large companies used to have over medium and small businesses is industrial espionage. Large companies could gather intel about their competitors and create the image they wanted, using digital media and help from ad agencies. Today, in the age of social media, the possibilities of expressing views, conveying messages and promoting a business are simpler for everyone.

Social networks are the basis on which we work, sell, buy and gather information. The Internet can be divided into two groups: (1) the viewers – information collectors; (2) the viewed – information providers. Most online businesses are medium and small in size. Medium and small business owners are the most viewed business owners online. Most mistakes are made by medium and small business owners. Now you, the business owner, are given the opportunity to play the viewer's game, collecting information free of charge, to your benefit.

Entering the World of Information Gathering

In this age of information, knowledge is power. That is why we collect information regarding the trends and habits of both groups and individuals. The human discovery that what we don't know far exceeds our knowledge has moved people to dedicate their time and energy to developing technological means for gathering personal and professional intel, in order to improve our understanding of our peer group's needs and desires. Professionals have developed numerous means capable of analyzing professional, military and social data and trends. There is artificial intelligence which recognizes people in photos and affiliation groups. Our smart machines can analyze and add data to present accurate graphs, **but they cannot understand our feelings, our intentions, our moods or our motives.**

Our ignorance regarding other people's feelings leads us to wrongly assess their intentions and emotions. Since the purchase process is emotional, understanding your customers' emotions is key to increasing sales and promoting your business. **Finding information in photos is like having the key to your customers' hearts.**

Many business owners are troubled by questions such as: what does my business look like? How do the customers view me? What's going on with my competitors? Any business owner would be willing to invest time and resources for the answers to these questions. The answer is already out there, and yet it is used by so few.

Usually, when asking business owners whether they would be willing to open their minds and learn something that may improve their profitability, I am answered with a hesitant, suspicious "yes". When someone promises you something good, it arouses suspicion and raises red flags and doubts: what's *behind* that promise? Business owners are inclined to believe that there must be something fishy about it, and they finally make a decision based on the questions: Will it pay off? Do I need it?

I'm not going to sell you a promise, but instead help you reveal what already exists within you – a language and intuitive tool for observation and information. It's a shame if you do not consciously use it.

How to Gain Intel on the Competition

You can't see it all. Ask yourself what it is you're looking for.
Photo: Shutterstock

Ophthalmoception

One of the most frustrating moments is when you're looking for the car keys while in a hurry, and you finally find them in plain sight. They were there all along, you *chose* not to see them. In professional literature, this phenomenon is known as "inattentional blindness". Something else is diverting our attention, blocking our sight, even though we think we see and remember everything and have a solid grasp on reality. When we have an opinion on a person or society, it prevents us from seeing the actual reality.

Here are some facts and food for thought about our sense of sight:

- We think that vision relies strictly on our eyes, but it's actually a combination of all senses, processed through the brain.
- The brain cannot differentiate between imagination and reality. Tests involving MRIs (Magnetic Resonance Imaging) show similar brain wave recordings when "viewing" imaginary images and actual pictures.
- Our brains repair and complete situations that don't actually exist (the Gestalt effect).
- When perceiving danger, it takes 3/4 of a second for us to respond. That is the brain's reaction time.
- When adapting to a new environment, our senses weaken and we see less data.
- The pictures we upload divulge our thought patterns.
- Seeing is a choice, not a reflex.
- Although we have a multichannel brain, it can only focus on one target image at a time.
- We believe stories and create corresponding images. The images settle in the brain as truths, entrapping us in a never-ending cycle of false reality.
- The way we interpret what we see is affected by our views and opinions.

Rules to Follow While Collecting Information from Images

When observing and gathering information, you should be aware of the fact that whatever you look at has an emotional impact, which can make you lose objectivity. Here are some ground rules you should adopt for gathering information on a regular basis:

✓ **Schedule information gathering sessions.** Set aside time for collecting business information on social media. Put it down in your calendar. A survey conducted in England[3] showed that two months of doing anything repeatedly turns actions into habits.

✓ **Learn your customers' activity patterns** including the hours during which they surf the net. For instance, a younger clientele uses the internet at different times than an older clientele.

✓ **You can't see it all.** Ask yourself what it is you're looking for. That is what you'll end up finding. What you find can be of great business value.

✓ **Avoid diversions while collecting information.** Gathering information in images is like meditating; everything becomes clear when all you do is observe.

✓ **Be accurate and maintain objectivity.** Look at each photo; write down exactly what you see, without interpreting emotions, memories, feelings, thoughts, ideas or connotations. Those usually have more to do with your own world than with the information in the picture.

✓ **Overcome your personal beliefs**, as they may affect your photo analysis.

---

3   **How are Habits Formed: Modeling Habit Formation in the Real World,** Published in the European Journal of Social Psychology by Phillippa Lally

✓ **Write down what you see and read it out loud.** The human brain responds similarly to reality and imagination. If you look at an object, close your eyes and keep picturing it, your brain will receive both, the tangible and the imaginary, in the same way.

✓ **Appoint an employee to be in charge of collecting information from images** or hire an external advisor to do so.

Before each meeting, I monitor the profile picture of the individual or organization in the social media. Prior to meeting them, I'm already well informed regarding the business and its managers. For example, I can discover who is behind each profile, their motives, their personal and group weaknesses, possible information leaks, and which organizations can become allies in collaborations to increase sales.

"The Emperor is wearing nothing at all!"

The famous tale "The Emperor's New Clothes" by Hans Christian Andersen, 1837, tells of an emperor who was obsessed with his clothes. He was told that there were two tailors who could make a special garment, invisible to anyone who is stupid or unfit for his position. The emperor gave them unlimited funds to create such a garment for him.

After weeks of "sewing" and the emperor's impatient anticipation of the wonderful garment, along with that of the entire empire, it was finally ready. The emperor summoned the entire kingdom to come and see his glorious new clothes. As he stepped onto the stage to present the one-of-a-kind garment, everybody acted impressed, so as not to be considered foolish or lowly. Only one small child cried out, "The emperor is wearing nothing at all!"

Illustration: Ariel Karmi Dror

Children interpret what they see innocently. Their box of memories is still empty and they are unaffected by prejudice or interpretations regarding what they're witnessing.

We adults aren't the same; our boxes are full of memories, opinions, views, prejudice, etc. This is why, when analyzing an image or photo, we must do so cautiously, while silencing all external "noise".

Images have a life of their own

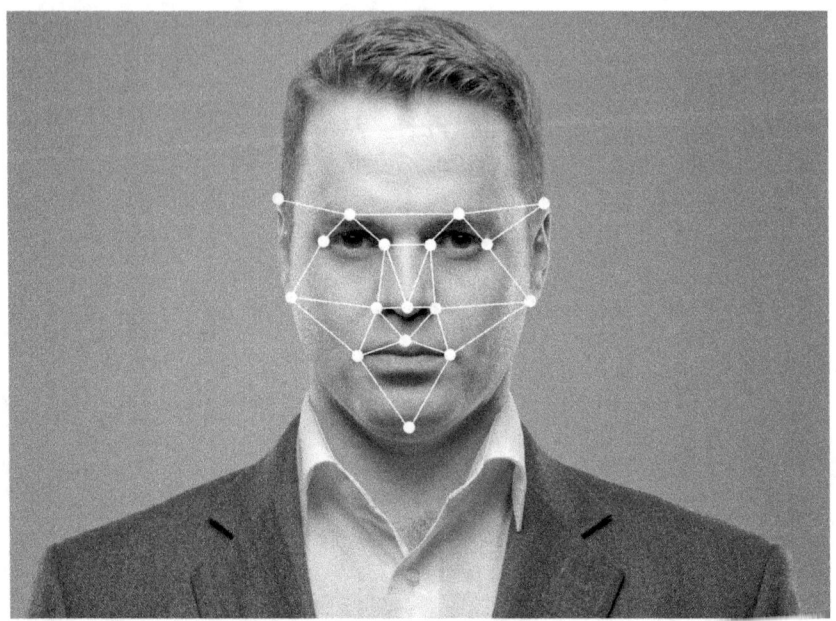

The Biometric Database
Photo: Shutterstock

Once our photos, including profile pictures or portraits, have become part of the Internet, we have no control over where they will appear and what they will be used for. We can discover our portraits deep within galleries and biometric databases or other directories, quickly finding that images have a life of their own and live on without us. By the time we realize this, it will probably already be too late.

The question, therefore, is how and when we will demand absolute ownership of our own faces. Will we soon be wearing hats? Covering our faces with lace? Taking low-quality pictures? Maybe this demand will fundamentally change the way we take and view photos. **Our face is a valuable asset, and we're giving it away freely to anyone who wants it.**

Portraits Reveal Hidden Identities

Sir Francis Galton, 1822-1911, was an English polymath, scientist, naturalist and inventor of the Eugenics philosophy. He is one example of a researcher who based an entire theory on collecting people's portraits. Some say that his research was the basis for modern day facial recognition systems; others, that his ideas served as the cornerstone of the Nazi racial theories.

Galton believed that portraits could serve as proof for the biological theory he named "Eugenics" (from Greek: "well-born race").

Genetics, so Galton claimed, are what dictates a person's "success", rather than life experiences as many believe. He asserted that, using photos, an observer can connect a person's inner being with his/her appearance.

His main thesis was based on the ability of photos to reveal hidden identities, which can be exposed through physical resemblances between any person and a group sharing similar physical and mental traits, which he claimed affected their expressions.

Out of this concept, Galton devised the idea of creating a device which scans the surface of human faces and divides them into 30,000 different coordinates. These coordinates would then be entered into an algorithm, which would indisputably affirm his research.

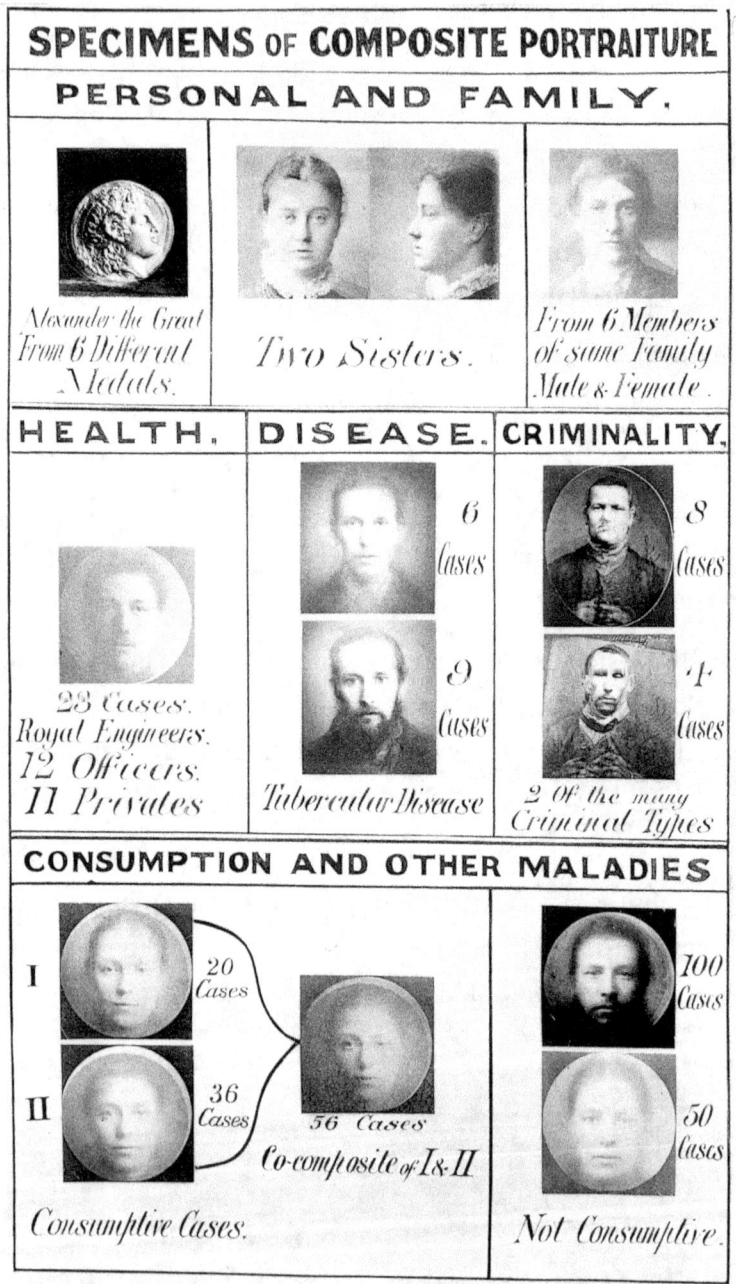

An example of Galton's work.

Photo: from "Inquiries into Human Faculty and its Development", 1883

Defense against Data Leakage through Photos

As already mentioned, people are unaware of the fact that they divulge information of a professional and personal nature when uploading unaudited pictures. The human need to share and tell overcomes our need for privacy. Using information about your competitors, you can gain the competitive edge.

During the opening of any lecture or meeting with executives, I alert them to how most people are unaware of the information contained in their photos. I usually hear things like: "What's the big deal, it's only a picture;" "No one looks at it;" "I have nothing to hide;" "The pictures I post are irrelevant." Then, to their astonishment, I perform a simple examination and reveal professional and personal information I've collected in advance from photos uploaded by them and their acquaintances.

This creates a discomfort, causing them to act quickly to stop the information leakage and improve their business image. Since most organizations don't have the huge budgets that large corporations do, I give them a few pointers that, if followed carefully, can achieve positive results within a week.

What can be achieved by collecting information from a social network profile, and why is it necessary for your business?

Below are a few rules which will help you defend yourselves against data leakage through images:

- ✓ **Awareness.** Make your peers aware of the abundance of personal information found within photos.

- ✓ **Don't "auto-share".** Avoid posting images online without careful consideration. Examine the information contained within.

- ✓ **Background check.** Check the photo's background for personal or classified information, such as bank statements on your desk or a list of competitors on your bulletin board.

- ✓ **Minimal caption.** Give your photos a title, but don't specify the name or location of the project.

- ✓ **Service or disservice?** Ask yourself whether the image promotes your business goals or impedes them.

- ✓ **Candor in moderation.** Exude sincerity, but don't divulge unnecessary information.

I believe privacy to be an important value. It is one of the reasons I have written this book: piquing your awareness. Using social media for your business brings with it great opportunities for international exposure and increasing your customer base, but it can also be dangerous, because disclosing professional and personal information can harm both you and your business. Every day I come across businesses that have evolved and have managed to increase their turnover through social networks; but alongside those, I also come across businesses that have been harmed because they failed to follow the basic rules of conveying messages and collecting information.

The few business owners who are aware of the information found in pictures choose the extreme option, ceasing to update or upload pictures at all. Overprotecting your business in social media may make it look detached or out of date. Your customers want you to engage them in visual dialogue. In order to maintain your privacy while still using the visual language for sending accurate messages that promote your business, you must understand the rules of this language. No one is immune to having their information collected, not even experts on the matter like myself.

Chapter Four:

From Theory to Practice

Photo: Shutterstock

Applying the Pareto Principle in Photos

The Pareto Principle, also known as "The 80-20 Rule" is a universal rule-of-thumb created by Italian economist Vilfredo Pareto. The principle creates a rough division pattern that has been applied to business, social studies and nearly any area of life. The principle states that, for many events, 80% of the activity comes from 20% of the sources. It helps distinguish between key and trivial factors.

In the field of gathering data, less than 20% of the information will be key to understanding the big picture. You need to identify the main factor within the image, give it your full attention and understand the visual codes that are conveyed through it; for instance: religious, political and cultural indicators. They will be represented by symbols, such as a flag, a family portrait, a wedding ring, the background skyline etc. This is also the case when *you* wish to convey a message through images. In order for your message to be received and "get the job done", you must carefully choose symbols that send the message in a simple, accurate way, and place them in your frame.

Although Pareto's numbers are not always precise, the simple truth behind them easily clarifies the principle.

An important tip: since images contain a lot of information in the background, apply the Pareto principle in order to crack the encoded information and convey an accurate message. When reviewing the photo, try to understand what the main symbol is: it will normally take up to 20% of the photo frame. Once revealed, the key symbol will be the key to understanding the picture's main message. Further details on this subject appear later in this chapter.

How Alex Moved a Mountain - a case analysis using The Visual Code and the Pareto Principle.

Alex, the rock and the mountain
Photo: courtesy of "Alex"

I sat in the last row of the auditorium, looking attentively at the lecturer, who wore an impressive business suit. His body language conveyed confidence and determination. He spoke eloquently, in a riveting tone of voice, and the crowd was his.

The lecturer was Alex, an international marketing advisor and hi-tech company manager in his mid-40s. "This is an interesting way to start a meeting," I thought.

Once the crowd had dispersed, we sat together at the end of the empty auditorium. There was an obvious disparity between the man who had just been on stage and the man sitting in front of me. Alex asked that we meet during the conference. He said he was having a hard time bridging the gap between his success and his feelings. Pointing at the stage, he began, "In spite of all this, I'm unfulfilled. Something in my interpersonal communication with my managers isn't working. I have ideas, but they don't pan out. I don't understand what is hindering me from penetrating the glass ceiling," he said. Alex could not describe his problem with words. However, the pictures he had sent me a week earlier, as per my request, *did* shed light on the source of the conflict, as well as its solution.

His picture, entitled "me", caught my attention. I chose it as the source image. This image reflected the source of the issue, highlighting it through visual symbols.

I looked at it. Alex was standing in the center, wearing traveling clothes, carrying a backpack. In the background: a mountain, a car and a rock.

Additional data derived from the photo:

1. In the photo, Alex is about 1/20 of the photo's size (see the Pareto Principle in photos.) this means that, either consciously or subconsciously, he chose to provide most of the information in the background.

2. When dividing the photo between the right and left sides (the right side of the photo normally being the practical area), Alex appears to be "carrying" the rock with his right arm. The rock

is heavier than what you would assume this man could carry, yet his body language exudes capability, which hints that Alex is a highly capable practical manager.

3. On his left (widely considered to be the emotional area), his free hand seems to either be open or asking a question. The answer to this question will usually be found in the background.

4. In the background, to Alex's left, there is a car. The car is blocked by a mountain and there is no paved road. As the car appears on the left, we interpret the symbol as pertaining to Alex's emotional side, indicating a possible personal and emotional conflict.

After the initial examination and writing down the objective data within the photo, I moved on to the next step, locating the picture's emotional contexts, codes and symbols. The car, for example, symbolizes movement, freedom, reaching a goal; the rock conveys gravity, an emotional journey; and the mountain represents a yearning for the summit, climbing to the top, moving mountains.

The key symbol reflecting a person's problem may reappear in that person's photos in different shapes and sizes. This specific photo contains little stones, a rock (behind Alex's back) and a mountain – three different symbols from the same symbolic world.

We reviewed Alex's conduct, finding that there was a gap between his inner vision and the way he managed his organization. Moreover, there was a communicational gap when conveying ideas to his managers and employees. Alex was a hands-on manager, prone to taking on more than he could carry (much like the rock in the photo). He didn't have time for new solutions and had reached a dead-end in his relationships, both with his employees and in his personal life (much like the car in the photo).

In order to best describe the situation and its resolution, I chose a quote by Confucius (The Analects): "The man who moves a mountain begins by carrying away small stones." For Alex, who couldn't find the words to describe or understand his conflict, this was a defining moment. For the first time of his life, he was able to see his thoughts mapped out in the photo he chose. There was no more need for words – Alex understood.

That same week, Alex took a day off and set time aside to plan and ponder. Shortly after our meeting, he sent me an impressively detailed plan for his continued personal and professional development. Alex had decided to move mountains! He began with the small stones, making time to think and learn privately. He returned to his Karate studies and dove into learning interpersonal communication through images.

During one of our last meetings, Alex told me about a substantial change in his personal and professional life. He said that he routinely uses the information gathering technique. Today, he is an international Senior Lecturer.

The Visual Code – My Secret Tool for Gathering and Analyzing Information from Images

The tool you are about to read about is my 'holy grail' of collecting and analyzing information in the visual world – pictures and photos. Using it not only enables you to analyze your business competitors' photos and convey messages through your own, but to prepare for interviews and even find a romantic partner.

This tool is designed as a research tool, beginning with the image frame (whether there is a title or caption), moving through the accurate data which appears in the photo (characters, objects, angles, lighting, etc.), interpretation (what each factor symbolizes), metadata (information regarding the photo's context, circumstance and photographer), and ending with conclusions.

Here are details on how to use this tool:

Caption

✓ Has the photographer added a photo caption? For instance, "Microsoft employee outing".

✓ What does the caption tell you?

✓ Write down any unclear terms in the caption (if any) and try to interpret them.

✓ Do you know the date on which the photo was taken? Is the date significant? For instance, July 4th –US Independence Day.

Data collection – what do you see?

Describe as many apparent details as you can:

✓ **Characters** – the number of people, ages, attire and dress code, expressions, demeanor, relationships (couples/coworkers/friends), and how the photographer chooses to present them (size/lighting/ position)

✓ **Photos and diplomas** – what are the images in the photo's background, and what can they tell you?

✓ **Objects** – size, shape, meaning, symbolism, use, and relationship with the characters.

✓ **Buildings** – size, shape, materials, style and design, function (office/home /hotel).

✓ **Fauna and flora** – quantity, order, organization, placement in the frame.

✓ **Angle** – point of view, camera angle, distance from the subject, frame limits (what's inside and outside the frame).

✓ **Sharpness and contrast** – which parts of the image are clearly in focus? Those are usually the objects that the photographer wishes to emphasize.

✓ **Detail placement within the frame** – colors, lighting, composition.

✓ **The shot moment** – was it taken in motion, or while standing still?

✓ **Shapes** – can you see any geometric or organic shapes?

✓ **Lighting method** – is the lighting natural or artificial? (sun, moon / light bulb, flash, candle)

✓ **Lighting direction** – the light indicates the general direction. Pay attention to the contrast between lit and shaded areas, as an indication of the time in which the photo was taken.

✓ **Off-frame** – can you imagine what's happening outside the frame's borders?

✓ **Picture and frame relationship** – a glance at something beyond the frame, lines leading to the frame's borders, cropped objects, etc.

✓ **Dominating factors** – what draws your attention? Close your eyes, open them again and look at the photo. What is the first thing to steal focus? This exercise can surprise us, causing us to see that the subject is not always the point to which our eyes are initially drawn. The photo's meaning may change when reopening our eyes.

Interpretation – what does it mean?

✓ Revealed and concealed messages, meaning.

✓ Recognizable symbols.

✓ Cultural and social signals.

✓ What are the characters doing?

✓ What are the characters feeling?

✓ Relationships between characters.

✓ Depicted ambiance.

Metadata - what is your external information regarding the photo?

✓ The event or context in which the photo was taken - an article, a title, an event (elections, conference, vacation).

✓ Previous information regarding the photographer and circumstance.

Conclusions - what are your insights?

✓ What is the reality captured in the photo?

✓ What are the views and values illustrated in the photo?

✓ How does the photo make you feel?

Gathering Information for Hiring Employees - *a case study*

A text message was sent to me, reading, "I'm in Israel, could we meet tonight?"

John had heard about the tool I use and decided to test the method's effectiveness in manager recruitment. He sent me a photo of a man named Robert, who he intended to hire as Head of Marketing in North America. It was a position which required creativity and thinking outside the box.

In the photo, Robert was seated in an office, looking directly at the camera, his head slightly turned to the left, emphasizing his grip on a MacBook laptop, raising an iPhone in his other hand. He wore a striped, outdated shirt, and seemed like a decent, pleasant, fatherly man. His body language indicated shyness and discomfort in front of the camera. The emphasis on the electronic devices in both hands indicated a lack of confidence in his abilities, or a problem with his professional marketing skills.

Though Robert seemed to be a pleasant person, the type who could get along with anyone, the creativity required for the job was not his strongest suit. The data in the photo was distinctive, but I decided to go a little deeper. I easily found his Facebook and LinkedIn profiles. His profile picture was the same one he had attached to his CV, indicating fixation and a lack of creativity. His Facebook profile was abundant in family photos of birthdays, along with photos of him with his wife, corroborating his conservative views. "He's not right for Head of Marketing" I said, "However... you're also looking for an office manager, right?"

"Yes," John replied.

"He's your man," I said decisively.

This was one of those cases where everyone could benefit. The man in the photo would have struggled to meet the creative challenges of marketing the new product, and his chances of success were slim. However, he could definitely serve as a safe anchor for the team and a reliable office manager, who would help create a pleasant atmosphere. John eventually hired Robert as his office manager. It was a win-win situation. John gained a dedicated manager who was fit for the position, and Robert got the job best befitting his talents. Robert has been successfully managing the North American office for over three years now.

To summarize, companies invest a lot of time and energy in selecting employees and managers. Sometimes, browsing through applicants' social network profiles can provide quality information which can contribute to understanding their skills.

Chapter Five:

No 2nd Chance at a 1st Impression

Photo: Shutterstock

A Meeting in Pajamas

ould you consider attending a business meeting unshaven,
wearing an old T-shirt or pajamas? I suppose you wouldn't.
However, bad profile pictures are not a figment of my imagination;
they can be seen every day on social networks.

When going to an important meeting in the business world, we want
to look our best, adhere to the appropriate dress code and be well-
prepared. These meetings are usually with one individual or a few
people. Why wouldn't you prepare for meeting thousands online?
Why would you upload a profile picture without carefully considering
the significance of its message? Often, people choose to upload what
they believe is the best photo in their gallery. Then, due to the (often
unbearable) technological ease of use, inappropriate images that fail
to serve us, or are even harmful and cause us to miss opportunities,
find their way into our online profiles.

Whenever people meet, whether in the virtual or tangible world,
there is an exchange of messages, creating the first impression. This
impression is not conveyed through words, but rather through codes
and symbols. During these meetings, we look for two main traits in the
person in front of us: **reliability and capability.** We try to determine
their skills and intentions toward us.

During a face-to-face encounter, we can process nonverbal information such as facial expressions, tone of voice, physical gestures, attire, eye contact and physical proximity. These indicators enable us to see intent and motivation level, feel whether they are nervous or relaxed, attracted to us or repelled, as well as their level of involvement with the interaction.

However, during a virtual encounter, it is impossible to rely on non-verbal communication in order to better understand the other person; therefore, the first impression is based on the message conveyed in the profile picture and additional photos. Virtual encounters are brief, often lasting no more than a few seconds. During this short time, you want to leave the right impression and cause the viewer to stay on your page.

Research shows that people who see a profile picture for the first time form an opinion about the person in it within less than a second.

Therefore, in your profile picture, you must be prepared for a meeting with the viewer just as you would be prior to an important business meeting. The only difference is that you need to prepare before each business meeting, whereas you only need to prepare once for a virtual meeting.

Choosing Your Profile Picture

Pause to think before choosing your profile pic.
Photo: Shutterstock

Choosing and uploading a profile picture is a routine part of our personal and professional lives. Many business owners fail to see the significance of it. During meetings, I often hear, "We have an excellent product, wonderful service, and the quality speaks for itself." "Great," I reply, "but you're not the only one in the field." In this competitive world, you should be using the right picture to convey the appropriate message for your business, thereby gaining the competitive edge.

Using imagery in online advertising is essential. The internet is a visual medium, and an attractive photo is the best way to tell a story or draw the readers' attention. Please note: you should be careful when uploading any photos without the permission of the subject or photographer. Using someone else's picture without their permission isn't only wrong, but illegal (copyright infringement).

Is there an optimal profile picture? In my experience, various elements in the profile picture affect the public's choices and emotions. The right photo will directly affect the customers, their decision to either buy your product or not, whether or not and they become your faithful customers and follow your page.

Your profile pic should make the viewer believe in you and want to do business with you. Before choosing an existing photo or taking a new one, it's important to know what platform it is intended for. A photo taken for LinkedIn, for instance, will be different from one taken for Facebook or Instagram.

Make preparations: write down the main message you wish to convey about your business. Understanding the message will help you choose the right photo.

The Photo that Changed the Campaign

The Canadian Prime Minister, Justin Trudeau, Performing the Peacock
yoga pose. Photo: Greg Kolz
The original photo was published in color.

How could one photo change an entire campaign?

Looks can be deceiving, and lead you to attribute someone with qualities they don't necessarily possess. The Prime Minister of Canada, Justin Trudeau, is a young, tall and lean individual with a commanding presence.

Trudeau, the son of Canada's former Prime Minister, Pierre Trudeau, surprised many by winning the October 2015 elections, following a campaign focused on hope and optimism. His political adversaries attacked him, claiming he was "just not ready" for the job, and that his best quality was his full head of hair rather than his intellectual faculties.

The photo that changed everything

An old photo, re-tweeted by yoga Instructor David Gellineau, this time in black and white, (it was originally tweeted in color by Trudeau back in 2013), changed everything. In the photo, Trudeau balances himself on a desk using both hands, performing a yoga pose known as the "Peacock pose" or "Mayurasana". The viral photo changed the tone and presented Justin Trudeau in a completely different light.

Why was this, of all photos, so successful in making waves? Here is some data that will shed light on the photo's power:

In the physical aspect, this pose is difficult to execute and requires practice, proficiency and a high level of control.

In the symbolic aspect, according to the Hindus, the peacock represents powerful things, such as love and immortality. This is traditionally the pose in which the peacock attacks the snake (which represents evil, flaws and human weaknesses).

In the emotional aspect, it turns out that this skill may be hereditary. Justin Trudeau's late father, Pierre Trudeau, formally Canada's Prime Minister, who is thought of as the father of modern day Canadian identity, was photographed performing the same Peacock pose. Justin Trudeau is associating himself with Canada's history through his father. The symbolic message is: "I belong to a line of warriors; I am not one of those youngsters who have no respect for their past." His historical reference weakened his opposition's claims that he was too young and inexperienced.

Is there nothing this man cannot do?
Former Canadian Prime Minister, Pierre Trudeau, August 1970
One year before his son, Justin, was born.
Photo: Peter Bregg

What actually happened here?

The message that Justin Trudeau would fight for Canada was implanted within the viewers' minds. Just like the peacock who kills snakes to defend man, Trudeau would defend the Canadians against all evil. This gave closure to his father's legacy.

As mentioned above, every image has revealed and concealed messages. Trudeau's photo reveals the many layers that can be found within each image, which are a result of rules and cultural contexts that have taken root over thousands of years.

The messages in this photo

The revealed message: power, strength, impressive physical abilities.

The concealed messages:

✓ Black and white photos are a throwback to the past. While in office as Prime Minister, Trudeau's father was photographed in the same pose.

✓ Respect for the past, but with differences. The father is outdoors while the son is in a building.

✓ Both younger and older people are smiling in the photo. This reflects a positive intergenerational connection.

✓ Trudeau's feet are 'blocking' the face of an older, portly man. In the viewer's subconscious, this can be construed as a metaphor for Trudeau's conservative opponents.

✓ The picture raises a question which is also its key message: **Is there nothing this man cannot do?**

The small change that made a big difference

When the photo was published in the past, it didn't make nearly as many waves as it did when it was published during the electoral campaign. Why? Other than the timing, there was one other key factor which conveyed the message in the clearest, most effective way: **when the image was published for the second time, it was in black and white**, reflecting a connection with the past, maturity, experience and quality (people often define black and white pictures as 'artistic').

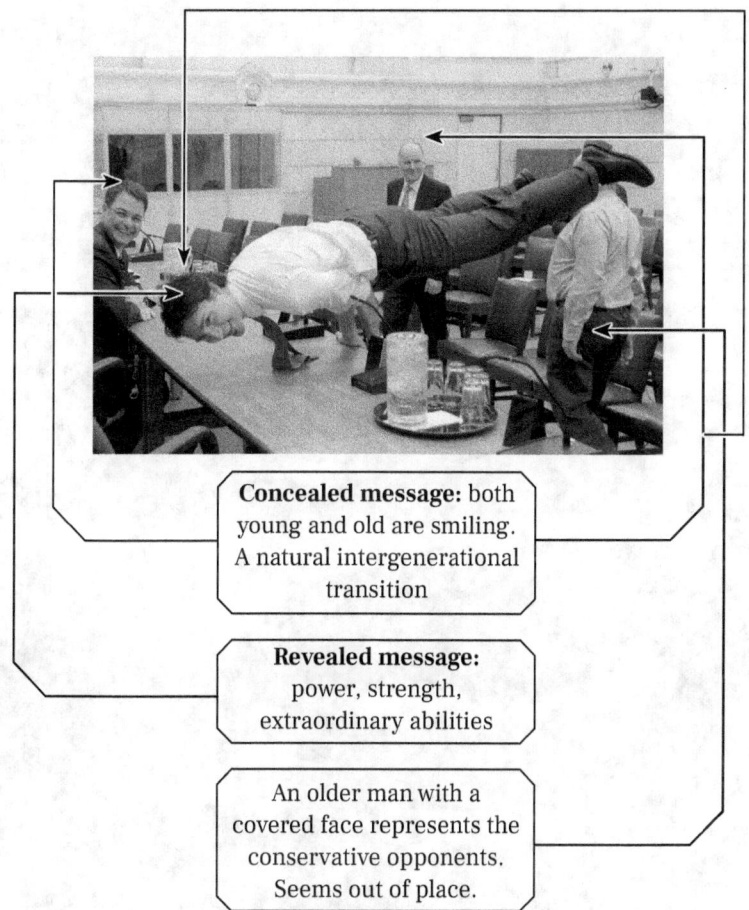

Concealed message: both young and old are smiling. A natural intergenerational transition

Revealed message: power, strength, extraordinary abilities

An older man with a covered face represents the conservative opponents. Seems out of place.

The viewer is exposed to both revealed and concealed messages.
Photo: Greg Kolz
The second time around, it was published in black and white.

Justin Trudeau wisely presented his true identity using the right photo, silencing his opponents. His powerful political identity shone through it, the public empathized with his inner truth and remembered the respect he paid to his private and public past.

Father (below) and son (above), doing the peacock pose.
Photos: Peter Bregg, Greg Kolz

Pierre Trudeau was one of the most popular Prime Ministers of all time. Among his achievements in office were officially adopting a multiculturalism policy in 1971 on behalf of Canada, which was the first country to do so, as well as the establishment the Charter of Rights and Freedoms and the patriation of the Canadian Constitution in 1982.

His son, Justin Trudeau, branded himself as his father's successor, often conveying this message through visual means.

After being elected, Justin Trudeau stayed true to his word and continued his hope and optimism campaign as part of his belief system. In promotional images for the Canadian Prime Minister, the next part of his campaign, tolerance and acceptance, is apparent.

Justin Trudeau was the first Canadian Prime Minister to join the Pride Parade, Toronto, 2016.
Photo: rmnoa357, Shutterstock

It can be presumed that, barring any unusual surprises, Trudeau will continue to lead Canada as Prime Minister for many years.

The 10 Golden Rules for a Successful Profile Picture

Photo: Shutterstock

1. **Choose a picture of *you*.** Don't use a photo of a baby, a pet, something you found online or a picture of your ID. Note: the picture should be up to date, taken within the past two years.

2. **Don't use a logo** as a substitute for a photo. People want to see the person behind the business.

3. **Look at the camera and make eye contact.** People who look each other in the eye are more attentive. People whose eyes were hidden by sunglasses, hair, a shadow or a hat, scored lower than those whose faces were revealed.[4] The more people like each other, the more they make sure to keep eye contact. This is also true when looking at another person's photo.

4. **Don't open your eyes too wide**, as it expresses vulnerability, fear and uncertainty.

5. **If you smile – show some teeth.** A closed mouth smile arouses suspicion. A toothy smile conveys optimism, health, happiness and ease. I recommend that my customer practice their smile for a few minutes before important meetings and photos.

6. **Slightly turn to the side**. A shaded jaw line creates an amicable feeling, much like standing in a slight angle, rather than frontal.

7. **Formal apparel is very effective**. The recommended attire for both men and women is a light, buttoned shirt, topped with a dark jacket or suit. This attire has been proven to be more effective than light or fashionable clothing.

8. **Frame your head and shoulders** (or from the waist up). Close-ups and full body shots scored a lower rating.

---

4   Look up Photofeeler – an app which offers unbiased feedback on your profile picture. It's based on a social media-wide vote, which rates pictures by three parameters: competence, likability and influence.

9. **Warm lighting**. Use warmer lighting (yellow light) for the photo. This color effects the viewer's emotions. The background should be light, as it scored higher on business networks.

10. **Avoid "noise"**. Try to avoid photos that are too dark or too colorful. Minimize your use of Photoshop and filters. Don't post any photos that have been aggressively cropped; they might come across as violent.

Do's and Don'ts in your profile picture

Who's hiding behind those glasses? Your customers want to know who you are. Photo: Shutterstock

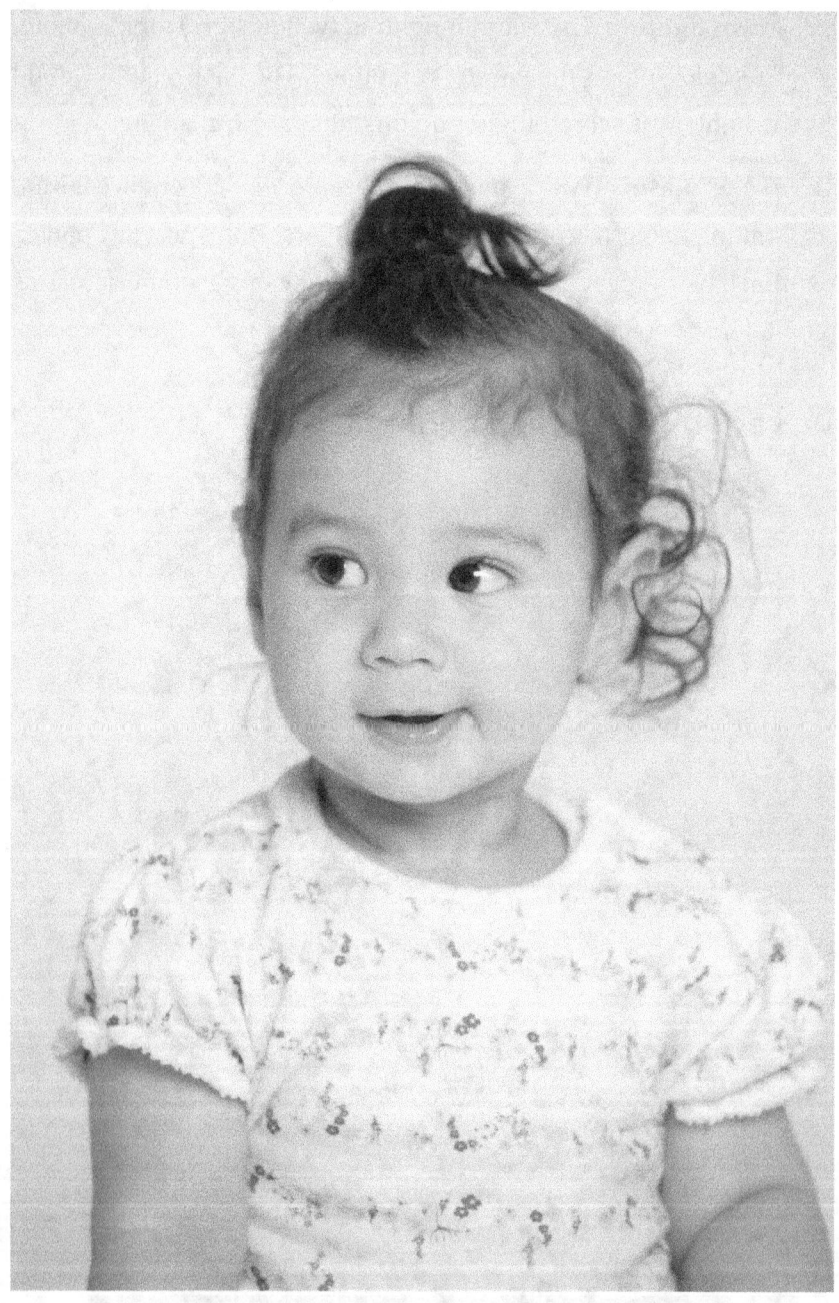

It may be the cutest baby in the world, but it isn't you...
Photo: Maya Karmi Dror

A toothy smile and slight turn to the side are better received.
Photo: Maya Karmi Dror

Formal business attire leaves the fastest impression.
Photo: Shutterstock

Sometimes, a prop helps emphasize the message: "I'm not *in* danger, I *am* danger". Walter White's trademark hat in 'Breaking Bad'.

Brian Cranston, Palm Springs, 2013

Photo: Featureflash Photo Agency, Shutterstock

However, even in this case, every rule has an exception. Uploading the right photo depends on each person's occupation, as well as profession. For example, I would recommend that actors use a dark or colorful background, and work in a prop associated with the character. Professionals whose work involves physical labor, such as technicians or electricians, would be wise to drop the suit and wear a uniform with their company logo.

Background by profession. Dark or colorful backgrounds are appropriate for actors.Photo: Shutterstock

Celebrity 'discounts' for choosing a profile picture.
Jeffrey Dean Morgan at the Watchmen premiere, Hollywood, 2009
Photo: Tinseltown, Shutterstock

While following the rules may help your business in conveying a clear message, some say that understanding them might be used for constructing a fictitious identity for various purposes. This is indeed one of the social network's phenomena. But by applying these rules, you, as a business owner can, enhance your professional visual image.

Once the photo has been posted, public reactions within the first few hours will indicate whether the image conveys the message you wanted.

How often you change your profile picture depends upon the platform on which it is displayed. On business platforms such as LinkedIn, the picture should be updated every two years, sending a message of security and stability to the viewer. On the other hand, a picture that is not updated for many years indicates a lack of credibility and hints that you are outdated. On Facebook and WhatsApp, you can change the profile picture more frequently. It is advisable not to change the picture too often, as it comes across as narcissism, fickleness and boredom.

In order to promote your business and improve sales, you must view social media as an opportunity to maintain your own permanent store, open 24/7, for an unlimited amount of time, commitment free. In order for your store to be profitable, you need to play by the platform's rules and be fluent in the visual language. The right profile picture, along with additional images which convey your message in a trustworthy and accurate way, will serve as your 'field sales agents'.

Using photos correctly can mean the difference between a successful business and a failed one. **In conclusion, remember – there is never a 2nd chance at a 1st impression.**

Mask Multiplicity and How it Serves You

Photo: Shutterstock

The word 'person' comes from the Latin word 'phersu' (mask). This semantic resemblance suggests that people are no more than masks. Real interactions require different masks. You can't make contact or connect with other people in real life, without wearing one mask or another.

Deepak's Lesson

In December 2007, I was given the opportunity to participate in a conference about combining effective leadership with spirituality. On stage, magically connecting spirituality and practicality, stood Deepak Chopra[5]. I sat eagerly in the audience; it was the first time I had the chance to organize and connect the different parts of my thoughts that had thus far been scattered.

During one of the intermissions, I stood at the far, slightly dark end of the auditorium, oblivious to the fact that Mr. Chopra, who was still too intimidating to come up and speak to, had been standing right behind me for some time. Both of us stood there in silence, observing the crowd. "Teacher," I hesitantly began, "I'm brimming with excitement and information that I can barely contain. Would you provide me with a sentence or an insight through which I can better organize the information I've accumulated?" He looked into my eyes and quietly replied: "What do you make of this man?" His eyes targeted a scrawny, bearded fellow with glasses, walking towards us.

I was at ease, pleased with the unexpected intimacy I had somehow formed with Mr. Chopra. I analyzed the man's body language, his intent and motivation and shared my thoughts about him. I was content with my knowledgeable demonstration. "Are you sure that's true?" His question curbed my enthusiasm. "You can only see one of his infinite masks," he added. "You, too, have many masks; give each of them their place and learn to live with them in peace and harmony". I understood. I can only see a piece of the picture.

The next morning, I lectured before an audience of executives about the significance of body language in images. Inspired by the previous night, I changed the order of my lecture, and downloaded

---

5   Deepak Chopra is an Indian-American author, physician and prominent member in the New Age movement.

a few Facebook photos of some of the participants an hour prior to its beginning. During the introduction, I asked Michael – one of the participating executives sitting in the front row – to stand up. I asked him if he is aware of what he conveys. Slightly flustered at my question, he replied, "Yes. I convey consideration and family values." I turned to the audience and relayed the question to them. "What do *you* think Michael conveys?" The replies were "strength" and "power".

At the end of the lecture, I showed them a picture I had downloaded, in which Michael was floating on the water, supported by a woman (presumably getting Watsu Aqua Therapy). When I asked what the man in the photo conveyed, the audience, failing to recognize their friend Michel in the water, replied with "weakness", "laxity" and "submission".

Weakness, laxity and submission - or power?
Photo: courtesy of the subject

"Well," I continued, after letting the crowd know it was none other than their friend Michael in the water, "Who is he really? A caring family man, a strong and powerful man, or a weak and submissive man?" They saw what I meant, and I saw what yesterday's lesson had meant – each person has a multiplicity of masks and identities, subject to how the observer interprets them.

People have trouble seeing the mask multiplicity in others. It's easier to see Michael as a lawyer or a pilot, and deriving who he is from that. It's difficult to comprehend that Michael is simultaneously a pilot, a father, a businessman, a friend, a competitor, an athlete and more. We have a multitude of identities within us, and social networks give us the opportunity express each and every one of them.

Same person – many masks
Photo: Shutterstock

Mixing Identities on Social Networks - *a case study*

During a meeting I had at his place of business, Danny, a businessman and entrepreneur, told me that his store chain was struggling to survive in an eBay and AliExpress dominated market. He angrily added a few derogatory insults aimed at social networks, ending with a defiant, "I'm done with Facebook." I asked him why, to which he replied, "Have you ever seen a sad person on Facebook?"

"Have you ever seen a sad person in a commercial?" I asked.

A simple examination of his existing profiles on LinkedIn and Facebook showed that his online business identity lacked cohesion, and that he had mixed his personal and professional personas. He posted photos of a private weekend vacation on his business page.

Furthermore, his employees had uploaded irrelevant materials that were damaging the message he believed in.

During our meeting, he was able to plainly convey his professional message: "fewer brands, fair prices, local stores and excellent service". "There," I said, "That is the message missing from your online business page." I knew that the qualities Danny had listed did in fact exist in his business reality, as well as in his stores; but at the same time I knew that no one was being exposed to it through the store chain's business page. During a staff meeting a few days later, in order to enhance the right message, Danny walked his employees through his credo and asked them to post stories and pictures about the excellent service at the stores, encouraging customers to write comments online.

Within a short while, the chain's Facebook page became more active; and several months later, Danny told me that their sales were steadily rising.

Monumental developments in the technological world have created a new breed of social business networks, wherein your mask multiplicity is naturally received and can even play in your favor, if you wear the right mask. Each platform has its own set of rules: you can be active in a number of platforms simultaneously, presenting a different side of yourself in each one. For example: your LinkedIn profile is your professional identity; on Facebook, you can keep your personal and professional pages separate; WhatsApp displays who you are to your close friends; Instagram shows your international identity; and on Pinterest you are your inner artist.

Your success depends upon three factors:

1. Understanding the rules for each platform

2. Launching activities and entering the platform using the right picture

3. Acting appropriately within the platform, in accordance with its individual rules

As a business owner, if you want to focus your marketing message, you must regard the human inclination for mask multiplicity and act accordingly. **You need to be aware of the differences between your personal and professional identities, expressed through the photos you upload.** Examine whether the photos convey the message accurately, and remember that your business self and personal self are not the same. Each character wears its own unique mask.

Wearing the Relevant Mask - *a case study*

I used to advise a large hi-tech company. In order to collect information, I met with the partners – a couple who was going through a marital crisis at the time. After a long meeting with the wife, she told me: "I know Uri, I do. No one knows him as well as me. I know things about him that nobody else does; if they knew... it's all a mask."

"Yes, you are his wife," I said. "You *should* know him from various angles, but since your customers don't intend to marry him, there is no need to expose them to irrelevant information."

The success of your business on social media stems largely from sharpening and polishing your professional identity.

Sometimes you must wear masks, which are reflected through the photos you choose to share. If you're having a hard time doing it yourself, consult friends or professionals.

Dissonance between the Virtual and Tangible World - *a case study*

Following one of my lectures to a large government organization, Bill, one of the managers, came up to me and told me that a co-worker of his, Jonathan, had asked for his help in transferring to a similar organization a few months back. Since Bill believed in Jonathan's skills and the two organizations had amicable relations, he was happy to introduce him to Tom, who managed the organization to which Jonathan wished to apply.

Several weeks later, Bill was surprised to hear that Jonathan wasn't hired for the job. During one of the management meetings, he inquired as to the reason why his friend was turned down. Tom replied in candor, "In the photo he sent, Jonathan was wearing a suit and seemed very professional; but he arrived at the interview wearing a colorful sport jersey, leading me to feel that he was unreliable, hypocritical and inconsistent."

"His truthful answer surprised me," Bill told me.

People won't normally admit to the deep impression an image can make, or how it can affect their decisions. They don't want to appear superficial, and so they claim that photos cannot convince them to form an opinion about the people appearing in them.

Below are three profile pictures from the same person's Facebook page. Who would you choose to do business with?

Photos courtesy of Amir Kahani

Photo: shitzu

Photo: Maya Karmi Dror

A disparity between your profile picture and your real life appearance makes you look unreliable and unformed. Prior to any meeting, you must consider the possibility that the person you are about to meet has already looked at your profile picture and formed an opinion before meeting you. You and your picture should be conveying the same message, and your body language and attire should correspond with what is in the photo.

A Simple Exercise for Bridging the Gap

I monitor the profile pictures of anyone I meet with in advance, as part of my work routine. During the meeting, I examine whether the message I'm receiving matches the one conveyed in the pictures.

Try this simple exercise: Before any business meeting or presentation, monitor your social network pages. Examine the dress code through which you have presented yourself. Memorize your message and business idea. Film yourself, using your mobile phone.

✓ Record your personal introduction on camera for 30 seconds, followed by the topic of the meeting for 1 minute.

✓ Play back the video and examine whether you look like your social network persona.

✓ Use this exercise to record your speeches before any lecture or presentation.

✓ Play back your videos to understand what can be improved about your facial expressions or body language. Make sure there is no disparity between your appearance in the videos and your social network persona.

This is one of my favorite, most frequent exercises. Customers send me videos in which they introduce themselves or their product, I send them my notes and they film and send again, after having read the feedback. In my experience, this is the fastest, most effective tool for noticeably improving presentations and body language. The purpose of this exercise is to create unison between the virtual world and real life.

If you struggle with the data analysis, have friends or family assist you. People understand body language intuitively and can naturally analyze pictures and footage.

If you're still looking for professional assistance, you can send me a video through WhatsApp or email. My number and email address appear on the first page of this book.

Chapter Six:

The Image of Success - What Do You Picture?

Photo: Shutterstock

From Images Online to Images in Your Mind

So far, this book has provided you with insights and tools regarding choosing the appropriate photos to embed in your social media pages, in order to convey an accurate, enticing and relevant message for your vision and business activity.

As I mentioned earlier in the book, our common language is the language of images. However, knowing how to post the right photo or accurately read the photos of others is not enough. First and foremost, we should think about our own images – the mental image.

We must examine which images/perceptions we hold onto in our minds, regarding ourselves and our place in this world. Do they stem from detrimental and castrating thoughts, or promotional and efficient thinking? If most of our mental images are born of coefficient thoughts – excellent. However, if they stem from anxiety, fear of success and wanting to stay in our comfort zone – we should take a closer look, understand what inhibits us from fulfilling our dreams and desires, and change it. Thus, the images will gradually shift from pictures of failure and fear, to those of triumph and success.

With positive mental images in our minds, not only can we apply the positivity internally, but better understand why winning images should be part of our external marketing.

My Own Image of Success

The heavy rain poured down on the starting line, forcefully whipping every part of my body. The water level rose above my shoes, making my feet heavy and my toes cold and stiff. Water cascaded down from my hat into my eyes like a pipeline, and I couldn't see a thing. But in my mind, there was one clear, weatherproof image: an image of me crossing the finish line. After a year of training and a stubborn injury six weeks before the race, here I stood at the starting line of my first marathon.

I'd dreamed of this moment for years, but had been paralyzed by fears, concerns and the unknown. One year before the marathon, I decided to face my fears. I asked myself a simple question: When picturing a marathon, what image comes to mind? Exciting images of runners reaching the finish line with their last bit of energy, crawling and groaning in pain, flashed through my mind. My brain was depicting the marathon through images of struggle and difficulty.

Most normal people I know wouldn't choose suffering, but they would definitely consider bearing it if it resulted in profit, pleasure and accomplishment. I could see that the problem was in how I perceived the marathon challenge. **I knew that I needed to change the image in my mind**, and so I publicly announced my plan to run, in order to cement my commitment. Running a marathon combines both physical and mental fitness. I devoted time to physical preparations through regular, orderly exercise. The mental exercise was more complex and less obvious, and so I read books and listened to lectures on the subject. But I failed to feel motivated, and the fear of running grew even stronger.

My concerns increased because I couldn't measure my mental preparation as I could my running advancement. After running for a couple hours, I could better understand my body's reaction, but how does one measure mental preparation? Six weeks before my first marathon, I encountered every long-distance runner's fear – an intensely painful knee injury. The doctors and therapists who examined me said that it was a borderline injury, leaving the decision to run up to me. As most of the training was already behind me, I knew it was a mental decision. I saw that the pain in my knee was a result of both my physical and mental states.

Physically, my impact was barely significant and came down to resting and icing my knee; but mentally I was able to have a greater impact, because I understood where my fear came from. It stemmed from not knowing what a marathon really was, or if I could handle it – a lack of knowledge which had generated doubts. I decided to train my mind, pumping it full of as much information as I could, in a language it can understand – images.

I knew I had to ignore my doubts and stick to my decision with determination. As of that moment, I started acting on two levels simultaneously:

✓ Physical preparation – regular training.
✓ Mental preparation –choosing my goal image, choosing my course images and mapping my route, using images.

A month before the marathon, I downloaded two photos from Google: (1) an aerial view of the track; (2) A photo of the finish line from the previous year. First, I studied the track. I divided it into three parts, using images to remember each one. After I could visualize the entire track, I started focusing on one image: **me at the finish line.**

One day before the race, I found out that my wife and daughters would be waiting for me at the finish line, changing my final image. Now, I visualized my loved ones waiting for me at the end of the track. The new image implemented in my mind on the day of the marathon was a powerful one, and every time I had a crisis threatening to overpower me, I thought of that image, which was stronger than my pain and surpassed my breaking point. I knew this was a race I would finish.

Me, crossing the finish line
Photo: RunnerScanner.com

Selecting the Image of Success and Choosing Images for the Road

From the moment we wake up each morning to falling asleep at night, we are on a never-ending rollercoaster of thousands of thoughts and experiences, translated into images we keep in our brains. We are the sole owners of these images; no one can see them but us. **We possess an unlimited ability to change any image by deciding to do so.**

Researchers testing two methods of accomplishing goals – writing down objectives vs. focusing on an image of success – found that people who had written goals had achieved them 39.5% of the time, whereas those who visualized their achievements were successful 76.7% of the time. People who achieve great success in their lives and reach their predetermined goals had most likely pictured **a clear image of success**.

When asking business owners about their image of success (or how they picture their goals in their mind's eye), I'm answered by flustered glances and even evasive body language, indicating that they had never thought of it. Some answer me using negation: they *don't* want to lose, take risks, work hard, step outside their comfort zones, be poor, sick or weak. They struggle to see the image they *do* want, never considering that the things they wish to avoid also become vivid pictures in their heads. The word "no" doesn't make you immune to a harmful image forming in your mind, pushing you further away from your goals.

People who see an image of failure	People who see an image of success
Picture many scattered images, or see none at all	Picture one single goal image
See problems	See opportunities
Accurately picture what they do not want	Accurately picture what they want
Their goal image involves a comfortable recliner and a cozy life	Their goal image involves hard work, and it doesn't scare them
Quit halfway through	Persevere and have self-discipline
Impatient pessimists	Patient optimists
Can't make decisions	Make fast decisions

People who have many images of success, or don't have one at all, **will probably end up serving those who have one accurate image.** You should remember that "only dead fish follow the stream". The river and current know all too well where they're going. Do you really want to stay afloat, letting someone else lead you there?

That's why choosing the image of success is a key component in achieving it.

Decision making is an important skill in both professional and personal life. When making decisions, our conscious memories of time – past, present and future – are significant factors. Past – what I have accomplished thus far, how things happened in the past; present – my ability to live in the here and now; future – expectations and concerns about what will happen. Too many pictures and thoughts about the past and future might delay our decision-making process, or bring it to a screeching halt. As a business owner, you make many decisions on a daily basis, decisions that may influence your organization's profitability, your future and the future of many others.

The right decisions are made through understanding the present image. There is a certain amount of courage required in making any decision, as it regards the future – a time which does not yet exist. We often make the wrong decision, and if we try to understand what led us to make it, we may see that during the decision-making process, our minds were filled with too many images of the past and future to see the image of the present.

For example: when examining a manager's compatibility with a role which requires acquiring knowledge, I test his ability to create new accomplishments without relying on past achievements. The past is a given, and contains both failure and success. If you repeat your past actions, you will probably get the same results. **However, if you want**

to make a change in your personal or professional life, choose a new image that excites you and makes you want to hit the road.

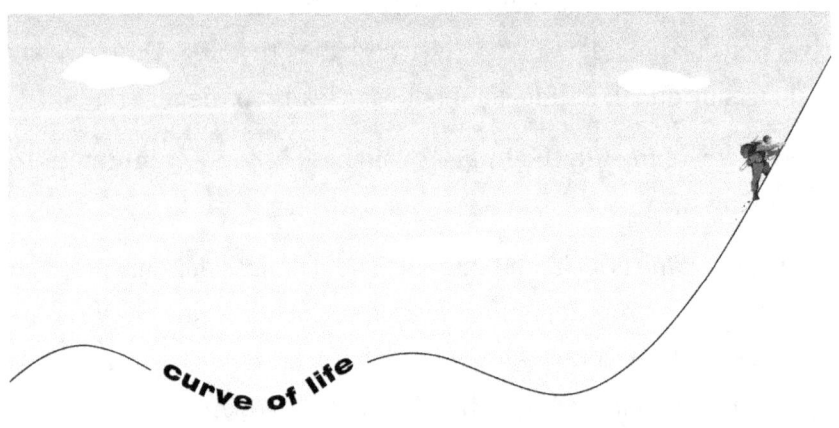

curve of life

What does our life's journey have in store for us?
Photo: Shutterstock

We only know the roads we have already traveled. We have no picture of the road still ahead. Choosing a goal image helps us focus and see the objectives we want to accomplish in the future.

A right decision is one that takes all of your inner wishes and desires into account. It supports your present life and serves your future goals and dreams.

Focus on a single, significant goal which matches your core values. Because we have multichannel minds, we think that we are capable of doing several things simultaneously. This is an illusion. We cannot effectively focus on two things at the same time. If you try to realize more than one goal, remember what Confucius said: "The man who chases two rabbits catches neither."

Don't start your journey before choosing a powerful image, which helps you understand the significance of achieving your goal and represents the final outcome. That is your image of success.

To reach your success, create checkpoints along the way, characterized by a certain place, time, etc.; and choose an image for each checkpoint, symbolizing your success in accomplishing it.

"Either I will find a way, or I will make one." ~ Phillip Sidney.

Pointers to help you construct the image of success and the road to achieving it:

1. Choose a single significant goal, one which makes a real change in your life.

2. Does the image you chose represent the benefit and significance of accomplishing your goal?

3. What are the checkpoints along the road to accomplishing your goal? Illustrate them, using images.

✓ Decision

✓ Starting image

✓ Halfway image

✓ Final image

Success is made of a series of journey images, ending with one single image: your image of success.

The Big Picture

"Once you find the source, you thereby know the product. Once you know the product, go back to preserve the source..."

~Tao Te Ching

So far, we've examined the pieces of the puzzle. Now let's look at the big picture. The flowchart below serves as the basis for conveying a message or identifying what stage an individual has reached. It's based on a combination of both modern and ancient views. The simple flowchart is an anchor, creating internal order prior to making a decision or setting out to achieve a goal.

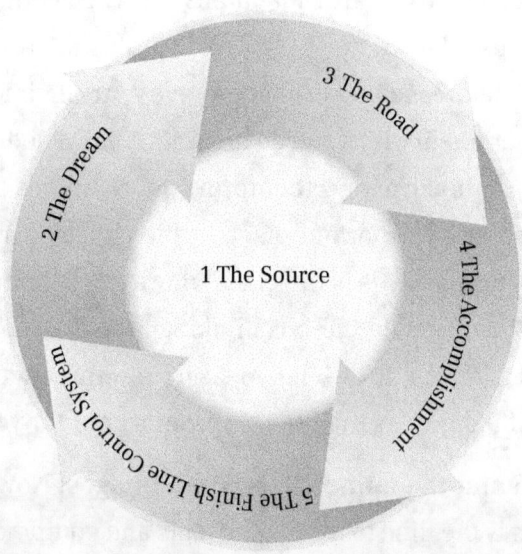

Five Images of Inner Order

1. **Start at the beginning – the inner image, the source.** You should create a firm base from which you conquer your goals and to which you return at night. Every one of us has internal core values, embedded in us since birth or acquired throughout our lives. Success comes from truly, boundlessly listening to who you really are. During hardships, when doubt arises, your core image is an anchor, and the one creating meaning. To find your inner source, relieve yourself of all judgment or limitation, and do not take instructions from anyone. Simply and honestly write down your inner desires: **who you are, what you want and what's truly important to you**. This will serve as the basis for building a personal and organizational vision and realizing your dreams. Once you have a firm base, you can dream and achieve any goal.

2. **Find new ideas. The dream/vision image** stems from the source image, from your true core values. What are your dreams? Do you have a vision? Find out what inspires you and write down your insights. Examine your true intentions and whether they serve your inner values. Make time to observe. Think simple and limitless thoughts. Before making decisions, give yourself time (according to the situation) in which you do nothing. A daily meditation is one of the most effective ways to improve your abilities at this stage. This is the most important place in the consciousness - where ideas are formed. This is the place where your Creative Quotient (CQ) lives and outside-the-box thinking is born. Lingering in this stage will allow you to develop ideas for new products and obtain important insight. As the final step, **set a goal for yourself.**

3. **The plan and the launch - the road images.** Now you have a goal. This is the time to collect the tools and equipment you need

for reaching it. Examine what you need in order to accomplish it. It could be collecting information, learning something new, organizing tangible means such as a car or plane ticket. Set three checkpoints, and create an image for each one (see details in Chapter Five). Focus on a single significant goal. If you're true to your core values, this stage will help you understand your motivation. Choose a powerful image which serves as your approval for attaining your goal.

4. **Accomplishment - the final image**. Once you're reached your target, enjoy your success, and share your feelings with others.

5. **Form a control system - ask questions**. Every stage is important, but this is the defining stage, because most people who reach it feel stuck and unable to change course. It's hard to say goodbye to an idea, a thought, other people. Sometimes people try to recreate past accomplishments in order to avoid striving for new ones. If you get past this stage, you can move forward. Create a control system. Ask questions and think how you can improve. Saying goodbye to a previous idea will give you room to create a new one.

Seeing Outside the Box – Creating Recurrent Success Through Images

Education as a Deterrent to Creative Thinking

I've often wondered why talented and successful people settle for the mainstream and choose to be average. Why are there so few who stand out in the crowd and take "the road less traveled"? I found one of the answers in a lecture by Sir Ken Robinson – an educator, popular lecturer, and international educational adviser. According to Robinson, the educational system operates out of the misguided belief that the worst thing one can do is fail or make mistakes. To see outside the box, you need to adopt the idea that failure is a necessary part of the journey. If you're afraid of mistakes, you will never discover new things; you will be left with the same static database of ideas and images.

The educational system is dedicated to satisfying the needs of the industrial world. It strives to find the shortest path to a solution, while trying to avoid unnecessarily wasting time and resources. In math, for instance, pupils are asked what 5+5 is. There will always be one answer: 5+5=10. However, in outside-the-box thinking, you can ask the same question and arrive at many answers. For example: ?+?=10. The answer is an infinite number of possibilities. The way you ask the question is what determines the solution.

Old-world educational systems have created metrics for success and failure. The accepted way of thought was: if I work harder, I'll be happier; if I scored a high grade, I will aspire to score an even higher one. The system measures and rates almost everything, including human intelligence. The IQ (Intelligence Quotient) is based on logical, spatial, mathematical and verbal questions. However, this metric, which was a monopoly for dozens of years, was only relevant to *some* components of the human skill set. A person with a high IQ could be chosen to manage a large system due to his/her ability to solve complex logical problems, but might have poor social skills. This is why the EQ[6] (Emotional Quotient) metric was created. EQ tests examine skills and abilities of identifying, evaluating and managing one's own feelings, as well as the feelings of others. Prior to the EQ, our eagerness to measure everything was contributing to mental fixation and making it harder to see things differently.

One of the new and interesting approaches for a broader vision was recently suggested by Prof. Bruce Nussbaum of the Parsons School of Design in New York.

Prof. Nussbaum, a renowned researcher and journalist who refers to himself as "The Innovation Guru", claims that, with all due respect to IQ and even EQ, the most important type of intelligence metric is the Creative Quotient – CQ. (See his excellent book on the subject.[7]) He claims that in order to succeed in life, and particularly in business,

---

6 For example: "Emotional Intelligence" by Daniel Goldman; Matar Publishing House, Tel Aviv, 1997.

7 "Creative Intelligence " : Harnessing the Power to Create, Connect, and Inspire"

one must show impressive creative skills, and that if we are not born with them – it's never too late to develop them.

"Many of us believe that creative people are visionaries who are ahead of their time," Prof. Nussbaum explains in his book, *Creative Intelligence.* "We've romanticized the notion of the lone poet starving in a garret or scribbling away by a pond far from civilization. We've come to have faith that science, neuroscience in particular, can explain why certain people are more creative than others, and we hope brain scan technology might offer insights about what the rest of us can do to become more creative. We may well have experienced fleeting moments of creativity in our own lives – but once it passes, we go back to life as usual, certain it was just a fluke."

The meaning of CQ, as Nussbaum articulated during an interview with Time Magazine on March 5th, 2013, is "**taking original ideas and scaling them into the creation of new products and services**. I really believe that we are all born with a capacity to be creative, and we get it beat out of us in a lot of the schools that we go to. We have to relearn it, and it's not that hard… Creativity is all about making connections and seeing patterns. It's not a light bulb that goes off in your head. Before that light bulb goes off, lots of things are happening. Lots of ideas. We need time to step back and make connections between those things."

In modern life, the distractions and various screens demanding our attention may be what prevents us from seeing outside the box and experiencing our own creativity. We're attentive to ideas, thoughts and states of mind displayed on screens, and they pique our interest in a meaningless, momentary manner.

This state, in which we are detached from ourselves, creates tension and uncertainty which may make us wrongly interpret reality.

On the other hand, when we look at the simple image of reality, we experience peace and a strong sense of fulfillment of purpose and achievement in our careers. **The first step of seeing the image of reality is the ability to see who you are.**

How creative thinking provided the team with an original solution - *a case study*

Creating new products and solutions stems from our ability to think and see outside the box. Creative people today are dealing with the challenges faced by groundbreaking pioneers: the need to explain and convince others of what they're doing. Sometimes, they battle alone, and they may experience difficulty and doubt along the way. If they wish to succeed, they must believe in themselves and know they are on the right path. Furthermore, they should select a supportive environment that empowers them.

Most people have yet to see that creative thinking isn't the privilege of a few; each of us has the ability to be creative. When I started walking down this road of collecting information and directing through images, I felt like a pioneer in the field. No one seemed to understand what I was doing or why. Many believed that I was taking unnecessary personal and financial risks. My environment encouraged me to stop and "get back on track"; my loved ones explained to me, using very sound reasoning, why I was wrong. But I kept at it because I believed in myself and knew I was on the right path.

I've encountered a lot of nay-sayers along the way, but occasionally I had the chance to meet organization managers with open minds and the ability to think outside the box. One of the people I am indebted to is David Cohen, CEO of the David InterContinental Tel Aviv Hotel, who provided me with the opportunity to work with his managers.

David is an internationally known CEO, one of the most prominent people in the IHG (International Hotels Group) and an inspiring individual. He believes in human-resource development, and is therefore constantly looking for ways and tools for nurturing and developing his staff. The first thing that caught my attention was that, along with his impressively professional speech, his managerial staff had the mandate to express their creative ideas and provide their own solutions. He does this through establishing 'think teams' on every management level.

Throughout years of accompanying the managers at the hotel, I came to notice that managers who gave vent to their creative thinking were those who achieved the best results.

One of those managers was Sotirios Ikonomou. When we met, he was a mid-level manager who had recently received a new division. He handled the complex challenge of forming a team of people from different countries and various cultures. In addition to forming the team, he needed to implement international procedures and bring the team to the highest standards of hospitality management.

Immediately upon our first meeting, we discovered a shared interest in photography. Sotirios told me that when he was fifteen, his father gave him a brand new SLR camera before a family vacation and said: **"Now is your time to learn, capture the moment and send your own message."**

As soon as he said it, we both understood that this statement embodies the concept of personal empowerment: a strong message and a powerful starting point, through which he could convey his organizational message.

Our first goal was "team unity". We started constructively paving the road. In addition to the excellent managerial tools provided by the hotel chain, we also used The Visual Code. I was happy to share with

Sotirios the creative part of the method for conveying messages through codes and symbols.

For instance, Sotirios wanted to convey a message of gratitude to the people on the team who worked behind the scenes and had a significant role in the division's success. He decided to make a movie documenting the housekeeping team, whose activity had thus far gone unseen (unlike the receptionists, sales people and waiters, who had been seen both behind the scenes and publicly).

The movie debuted at the hotel's quarterly cocktail party and was published online. It was very well received and made waves throughout the hotel, as well as the international IHG. Sotirios testified that he could see the results even during the first screening. He saw the housekeepers' proud looks. Throughout the following days and weeks, there was a rise in motivation within the division, proving that employee satisfaction translates to measurable value.

The Perfect Team
Film: Sotirios Ikonomou
https://www.youtube.com/watch?v=iVlSztSWJ0k

Aside from using films to unify and empower the team, Sotirios used gigantic posters he had made, showing his team against the backdrop of a movie or magazine (a background filled with international icons). The new world created in the posters sent the message – we are together in the reality we have created. The use of icons and symbols to empower the team worked. The posters, which were posted in the office halls, welcomed the staff each morning. The team felt proud to be part of the project and committed to the workplace and their roles within it.

The posters were successful in conveying the message: "together – we make the perfect team". After generating a positive environment for the team, Sotirios was able to implement messages and new protocol more smoothly than ever before.

I should note that films and posters are not a magical solution. However, they can reflect your thoughts and communicate them to others. Your actions are constantly compared with your messages by those around you. Your message comes across in a powerful way when your actions match what you convey in pictures or videos, because it makes you seem reliable. That is the cornerstone of any relationship.

The hotel's employees in a Hollywood film poster.
Photo and processing: Sotirios Ikonomou

Sotirios' success was derived from his willingness to go down a new road where no one had gone before, which required walking the extra mile in addition to the complex management of a diverse team. It was his creativity, his willingness to incorporate new tools, surpass fears, difficulties and doubts – which brought him success.

To summarize, using photos and videos in this case brought great results – a win-win situation for both the organization and the employees in a short period of time – because the concept of success became visual. **It's not enough to do the right thing. It should also be seen, to create the right ambiance in the organization.**

Since then, Sotirios has been promoted to the highest management level. Today, he a senior executive at David InterContinental. Below is a link to his original article:

https://www.linkedin.com/pulse/my-father-taught-me-use-camera-convey-feelings-pride-sotirios?trk_hp-feed-article-title-like

Outside-the-box training

In order for thinking and seeing outside the box to become a part of your daily routine, you should think openly, rather than automatically adopting existing formulas (even those found in this book) for happiness and problem-solving. Think independently, and always examine what works for **you**.

Carry an 'idea' notebook with you, and write in it on a daily basis. Don't be afraid of trial and error, and remember that each problem has many different solutions.

My own experience has taught me that one can practice and develop outside-the-box thinking. Here are some ways through which you can increase your ability to observe and see outside the box:

1. **Mental reinforcement:** Through daily meditative training; we train, eat properly, improve our bodies and try to better our lives in different areas. Weariness that overcomes us signals the body to rest, but our minds need restful breaks too. We have an ongoing stream of thoughts, images and emotions within us, which also need rest. Throughout the years, I found that the more I make sure to give my consciousness time to rest, the more my creative thoughts, outside-the-box thinking and observational skills flourish.

2. **Physical strengthening:** In order to maximize our physical energy, we must eat right, exercise and get enough sleep.

3. **Emotional energy:** In order to enhance our emotional energy, we need to surround ourselves with friends and family, share with them and include them in achieving our goals.

Yes, it seems simplistic, and you may have heard it in the past. But do you apply it to your life?

Change Your Life's Image by Changing how you See the World - *my own case*

The Survivor image

In 1989, I was making my way back to Cusco, Peru, following a prolonged stay in the Andes. Something in my journey had gone wrong, and I couldn't quite put my finger on it. I had been mugged for the fourth time! And the last mugging was different from all previous ones. The muggers weren't a gang of youngsters, a bunch of women disguised as Peruvian farmers in large cities, or an officer wanting to add to his salary by robbing tourists. This was an organized group of four muggers attacking my travel companion and myself. If it weren't for last-minute resourcefulness, I don't know where I would be today.

The long ride on the rickety truck gave me time to recreate the images in my mind and search my soul. Deep down, I knew that if violence was happening around and towards me on a weekly basis for the past six months, something in me, which I couldn't yet recognize, must be wrong. I decided to stop blaming external factors, such as geopolitical circumstances and statistics about the number of mugged tourists; I chose to take responsibility – figure out my role in the events and try to see whether I could affect and change my reality.

I'm not sure what led me to think this way, but as always, I was thinking in images. I asked myself what image represented each period of time in my mind. I started recreating my journey's images, from the moment I landed in South America.

The first image: Lima, Peru. I stood first in line before the giant plane doors, sharp, alert and ready for any predicament. On my back were 44 kilos of equipment – an improvised operating room, including syringes filled with anesthetics, a machete, and survival gear. I left feeling like I was on a survival quest, rather than a trip. I arrived in South America with an image planted in my brain, hindering me from seeing the actual reality around me. Every person I encountered was a threat.

The second image: Tel Aviv, Israel. About a month before I left, I met with the adventurer Yossi Ghinsberg, who was made famous by his inspiring book, "Back from Tuichi" (today, he is a popular international lecturer), to seek his guidance and get tips before my journey. When the meeting was over, he asked me to locate his friend – Luis Jetas– whom he had lost contact with. This was not a simple task, as it was prior to the social-media age, and looking people up on Facebook was not an option. I promised him I would find lost Luis, and left.

I was in my twenties, searching for meaning and direction in my life. The meeting provided me with the reasons behind my travel: (1) **A clear goal** – finding Luis. (2) **Value and meaning** – helping to locate a missing person. What I didn't know at the time was that once you've set a goal, the human mind selects an image which defines that goal. In fact, it's preferable to choose an image which has sentimental value, one that reminds you why you set out to reach it.

I didn't know then what I know now, as a result of writing this book: when you don't have your own image, you take it from other sources. The image I had subconsciously chosen was one that had had an impact on me back in high school – a picture out of Yossi's book, "Back from Tuichi", on the day he was rescued. His body was scrawny and haggard, his clothes torn and consumed by termites.

**The image of success (the goal) which was lodged in my mind –
Yossi Ghinsberg, as found by the rescuers.
Photo: Kevin Gayle**

I was too young to understand life's complexities, and had subconsciously chosen a photo of a man who had overcome the jungles and survived against all odds. This photo, which was already implanted deep within me, was the source of the events to come. It was a guide light in darkness, a beacon for a ship on a stormy sea. The photo dictated the rhythm to which I traveled and gave me the strength to make important, often irrational, decisions. It wouldn't be an overstatement to say that this photo played a part in my writing today. Don't get me wrong – I was never lost in the depths of the South American jungles. No matter what I encountered, it was always clear to me that I would survive.

I had but one picture in my head – finding Luis. The goal image was like a smokescreen over reality. I could see only that, and not what was in front of me. **Once you have a certain image of reality, you will find any justification to corroborate it.**

The plane doors opened, and rather than jungles, enormous snakes, coups and riots, short locals with slightly concerned expressions appeared before me. Even when one helped me unload my massive backpacks, I wouldn't let reality change what I wanted to see: I suspected that he was plotting against me. Danger lurked in every face and on every corner. I entered a local cab, where the short driver politely asked: "Where to?" "A hotel," I replied. "Which one?" he asked. I had no answer. The driver knew he was dealing with a Gringo (foreigner) who had no idea where he was (as I, in my mind, hadn't reached a destination, but rather an imaginary experience taking place in my head). Suddenly, it hit me – I've just arrived in Lima, I only know two Spanish words and I have only a general notion of somehow reaching Cusco. I didn't even have a map. The cab driver could take me anywhere and exploit my ignorance. Fortunately, my concerns proved false, and he drove me right to the Crystal Hotel, exited the cab and walked over to the kind receptionist to explain my situation for me. He gave me exact change and a polite farewell.

I was headed to Cusco. On the way, I rode past a breathtaking view, but I couldn't see a thing. I was on a mission – finding Luis. Two weeks later, I arrived at Cusco for the first time. When I asked small restaurant owners about Luis, I was referred to an old, small building in one of Cusco's back alleys. Curious to know what I was doing, a neighbor told me that Luis was a travel guide and had left on a very long trek, but he had no knowledge as to the destination. Since I didn't know where to look, I decided to carry on and return to Cusco in the future.

I left Cusco with a group of European and Canadian youth I ran into in a local pub. One month later, I left them and was alone on the road again, me and the picture in my head, looking for danger and ready to survive it. The story of the events along the way is yet to be written, but in the six months before reaching Cusco for the second time, I was involved in unpleasant mishaps and violence. I was mugged four times, spent days in a La Paz jail because I wouldn't bribe the guards, found myself running the streets in crowds, while soldiers and cops chased us, gunshots were heard and the smell of tear gas hung in the air. My trip had become a journey of survival and self-defense.

Disillusionment - changing my goal image

The soul-searching truck had finally arrived at Cusco, after days of travel and a realization that had thus far escaped me. When I got off, I saw something I hadn't seen in months: the people around me. I wanted to get closer, but I felt that I was making them both curious and afraid. The people in the city square looked at my huge backpack, with my machete strapped to its side. As I hadn't bothered to learn the native customs, I didn't know that publicly displaying my weapon was essentially challenging their social codes. I was the embodiment of the aggressive foreigner, invading their territory. Their eyes divulged everything I was to them.

An hour later, I was looking at the city square from my hotel room, knowing full well what I had to do. I removed a few essentials from my backpack and repacked them in a smaller one, went down to the square, unloaded my heavy backpack in the center of it and left, leaving a trail of curious silence behind me. The locals looked astonishingly at the Gringo who had abandoned his supplies, off of which several Peruvian families could live for a month.

I looked out the hotel window again as a crowd formed around my backpack, feeling that they understood me. I left more than my equipment on that square. I left the mental baggage which contained my blindness to reality, the metaphors and stereotypes I had packed inside of it. I left the picture of the survivor I had carried from home.

The next morning, I went to the ally in which I had met Luis' neighbor. The locked office was now open, and a pleasant man greeted me with a smile. I asked him if he was Luis. He was.

When I mentioned Yossi Ghinsberg, he immediately understood, and following a heartfelt conversation, we sat down together to write Yossi a letter. The ease and simplicity through which everything happened, from that day on, allowed me to me choose a different path. From that point, my journey soared to new heights.

Lighter in the absence of my heavy equipment and the wrong picture in my head, I was on the road once again. This time I was carrying only a toothbrush, a camera, one pair of jeans, one t-shirt, a little money, my passport and a mind open to sights, and free of confining images. I decided to get to know and understand the locals, and visit their villages; I decided to see the sights, breath in the experiences, and learn about myself and everything around me.

The climax of that year happened during one of my travels to the Amazon region. I was telling a joke to my local travel companions about my journey through the continent. The truck stopped, and another local boarded. He sat down, joining the lively conversation and my anecdotes from the road. One of the passengers turned to him and asked "Well, what do you think about our Gringo?" He looked flustered, leaned over to me and whispered, "Say, can you point him out? I don't know who they mean." "I'm the Gringo," I replied. His surprised look was a testament to the long way I had come, from landing in South America as a foreigner to becoming part of the local scenery.

The clouds begin to scatter

My trip taught me that I had to nurture my inner values and conduct myself accordingly. I learned how to observe independently and without mediation, and learn about myself and those around me through introspection. The next time I traveled, I had the goal image (where I wanted to go) and images for the road in my mind. I made sure they were always closely knit with my inner values. I allowed myself to see the simple, unfiltered reality, without mental images from home. This lesson almost cost me my life. I learned to give up many of the pictures in my head, which weren't created by me, but fed to me from an external source; pictures that used to dominate my consciousness. As soon as I cleared out the image clutter, I was free to make new connections and develop ideas. I felt that I could finally make the best of myself and maximize my contribution to my surroundings.

Closure

In June of 2016, I met Yossi Ghinsberg again, 28 years after our first meeting, and we had our closure. I was amazed to find out, in retrospect, that just as I had traveled to South America following his thrilling book, "Back from Tuichi" – he had traveled to South America following Henri Charrière's book, "Papillon".

We discovered that our experiences in South America were life-changing. We saw similar things. After our respective journeys, we both went on wandering for years. That is what led us to what we still do now – passing along empowering experiences.

Yossi Ghinsberg and I, June 2016
Photo: Belinda Ghinsberg

In reality, the seeds for this book were sown in South America.

I learned the meaning of the pictures in my head, and how to use them to empower and promote others, while Yossi Ghinsberg went "the whole nine yards". In March 2017, a movie entitled "The Jungle" will have its Hollywood debut. It's the story of his survival.

Epilogue

I hope this book has aroused your curiosity and awareness of the power of images in our lives, and the existence of the intuitive visual language within us. I hope that, after having read it, you will use this language to promote your business, as well as yourself. If you do so, that will be my reward.

If after reading this book, you understand the principles of the visual language, choose the images which convey an accurate message to promote your business, remove those which may harm it, collect information from images as part of your daily business routine - and most of all, dive in to improving your mental images - my work here is done.

You are welcome to write to me and share your insights and comments about the book. A wise man learns from anyone. If you would like to move forward and develop in this field, I would be happy to hear from you.

Yours, Yoni Dror
September 2016

Additional Credits & Descriptions

Page 43

LOS ANGELES - FEBRUARY 04 : Robert De Niro at the Handprint Ceremony at TCL Chinese Theatre for Robert De Niro, at 6925 Hollywood Blvd on February 04, 2013 in Los Angeles, CA

Page 45

Benicio Del Toro at the Los Angeles premiere of 'The Wolfman' held at the ArcLight Theater in Hollywood, USA on February 9, 2010.

Page 47

New York, NY USA - June 01, 2014: New York State Governor Andrew Cuomo attends 50th annual Israeli Day parade on 5th Avenue in Manhattan

Page 48

SACRAMENTO, CA - JUNE 01, 2016: Republican Presidential candidate Donald Trump speaks at a campaign rally in airport hanger in Sacramento, California

Page 49

New York City, New York, USA, March 30, 2016; Democratic Presidential Candidate Hillary Clinton walks onto stage at the Apollo Theater in Harlem, New York City.

Page 66

SAO PAULO, BRAZIL - July 9, 2014: Lionel Messi during the 2014 World Cup Semi-finals game between the Netherlands and Argentina at Arena Corinthians. NO USE IN BRAZIL

Page 72

SURATTHANI, THAILAND - DECEMBER 4 : The funeral of Lor Sae Yuk, the much-respected of Chinese-Thai people in Suratthani passed away at 102, on 4 December 2013 in Suratthani.

BETHPAGE, LONG ISLAND - MAY 7 2015: a formal viewing for slain NYPD officer Brian Moore, attended by thousands of police officers from North America. Family of Brian Moore escorted into funeral home

Page 83

WARSAW, POLAND - APRIL 17, 2016: Volleyball Champions League Final Four Zenit Kazan Trentino Diatec n/z Zenit gold medal winners champions confetti

Page 139

TORONTO,CANADA-JULY 3,2016:Justin Trudeau in 36th Pride Parade in Toronto. He is the first ever Prime Minister of Canada to walk the LGTBQ celebration

Page 147

Bryan Cranston at the Awards Gala for the 2013 Palm Springs International Film Festival. January 5, 2013 Palm Springs, CA Picture: Paul Smith

Page 148

Jeffrey Dean Morgan at the Los Angeles premiere of 'Watchmen' held at the Grauman's Chinese Theater in Hollywood, USA on March 3, 2009.

COUPON

50% OFF

A personal session with Yoni Dror

Phone: +972-52-2807505 • Email: yoni@yonidror.co.il

COUPON

30% OFF

A "Visual Secrets" lecture

Phone: +972-52-2807505 • Email: yoni@yonidror.co.il